MARK CUBAN:

The Maverick Billionaire

By Sean Huff

KEEN
publishing

KEEN PUBLISHING
Jacksonville, FL

The Modern Moguls Series

Entrepreneur, media mogul, celebrity and the ultimate sports fan... Mark Cuban is one of the most colorful and controversial billionaires of our time. A self-made man who has inspired millions to follow their own dreams.

"Mark Cuban: The Maverick Billionaire" is the first in the Modern Moguls series of biographical profiles, spotlighting the men and women who shape our modern business landscape.

Table of Contents

Chapter 1: The Maverick

Mark Cuban sits in one of the most high-profile chairs in entertainment. He's comfortable. Exactly where he wants to be.

A few hundred people in the room have their eyes affixed on him. Several cameras record his five minute interview, which will later be beamed to millions of TV viewers. On either side of him sit two A-list celebrities paying him their undivided attention.

This is Mark Cuban, the energetic, passionate technology genius who turned two companies into billions of dollars of personal wealth before he became a household name when he acquired the NBA's Dallas Mavericks.

With all the topics this interviewer could quiz Cuban about, he chooses to lead off the chat with a question about a disgraced baseball player and the leadership of Major League Baseball, a sport in which Cuban has no financial interest or presence.

Without understanding Mark Cuban, one might even wonder if he belonged on *The Tonight Show* in the first place. He was originally scheduled to appear two days before this particular Thursday night in August of 2013, but he was bumped by President Barack Obama.

To reschedule his appearance, Cuban had to rearrange his schedule, one that is jammed full, given the mogul's many business interests. And people will usually only subject themselves to late-night talk shows to shill for their movies, books or TV shows, none of which Cuban had to talk up on that program.

So why would *Tonight Show* host Jay Leno begin his interview with a basketball team owner by asking for his thoughts on how Major League Baseball handled superstar Alex Rodriguez's alleged use of performance enhancing drugs?

Because Mark Cuban has strong opinions on almost everything and he will express them without filter, seemingly regardless of the consequences. And sitting next to actor Robin Williams, the first guest on that episode, Cuban did not disappoint.

When Leno asked about Rodriguez's 200+ game ban for using performance enhancing drugs, Cuban accused MLB Commissioner Bud Selig of waging a personal vendetta and not following the league's own rules on handling drug violations.

"Horrible. I think it's disgraceful what Major League Baseball is trying to do to him. It's not that he doesn't deserve to be suspended, he does," Cuban said. "But they have policies in place. First-time offenders, 50 games. Second time, 100... 214 games? That's personal. And I got to tell you, my experiences with Major League Baseball -- and after all this there's no chance I'm going to be able to buy a team -- it's basically become Bud Selig's mafia. He runs it the way he wants to run it."

He went on to accuse the league of doing "everything possible" to keep him from buying the Texas Rangers in 2010.

"They had lawyers in there trying to change the rules, they had people trying to put up more money. It was horrible," the billionaire blasted.[1]

Cuban's words appeared in hundreds if not thousands of blogs, news reports and sports columns the next day. Whether he intended to or not, Mark Cuban received a whole lot of publicity.

And if you think he only expresses opinions when there's little risk of punishment or consequences, you don't know Mark Cuban.

---

[1] "Mark Cuban Rips Bud Selig on A-Rod Suspension on Tonight Show." Huffington Post, August 9, 2013. Retrieved from http://www.huffingtonpost.com/2013/08/09/mark-cuban-bud-selig-a-rod-suspension_n_3731984.html

Look up the word 'maverick' in the dictionary, and the definitions fit Cuban in nearly every respect. The only thing missing is the mogul's photo next to the entry.

A maverick is defined as "a lone dissenter, as an intellectual, an artist, or a politician, who takes an independent stand apart from his or her associates." It can also refer to "a person pursuing rebellious, even potentially disruptive, policies or ideas."

Some of the synonyms provided for maverick include nonconformist, individualist, free thinker, loner, rebel, and loose cannon. Aside from loner, all of those labels surely apply to one Mark Cuban.

The "lone dissenter" aspect of being a maverick is something that Cuban considers good business practice.

"Wherever I see people doing something the way it's always been done, the way it's 'supposed' to be done, following the same old trends, well, that's just a big red flag to me to go look somewhere else. When you've got 10,000 people trying to do the same thing, why would you want to be number 10,001?"[2]

---

[2] What I've Learned: Mark Cuban. Esquire.com, November 17, 2008. Retrieved from http://www.esquire.com/features/what-ive-learned/ESQ1206BBCUBAN_182_1

Being rebellious and disruptive supports the Mark Cuban brand. It's an identity that has become known in multiple circles for eschewing authority, challenging the status quo, and speaking "truth to power" in almost every institution.

Those traits are often portrayed negatively, but Cuban has created a persona that would make a worthy protagonist in a best-selling novel. What makes Cuban a likable figure is that the persona is genuine.

He's the same person no matter the setting. One would be hard-pressed to find any hypocrisy in his myriad volumes of blogs and quotes. Cuban is a rarity in today's society: an anti-establishment billionaire. Over the years he has criticized many of the institutions that people hold sacred.

Mark Cuban would probably say the reason he is wealthy is because he's always stood on the opposite side of the elite. Even though he now has money, he's not about to join them.
That includes his fellow owners in the National Basketball Association.

While his peers act the part of dignified team owner, Cuban acts more like his customers, the fans. And if there's one downside to owning the Dallas Maverick for Mark Cuban, it's that he has somebody to whom he has to answer.

No, David Stern is not his boss. But the commissioner of the National Basketball Association and the league he has presided over for 30 years has rules. And Cuban frequently breaks those edicts, especially ones that forbid public criticism of the league's referees, to the tune of several million dollars in his dozen years of team ownership.

Following a meltdown during the 2006 NBA Finals that cost Cuban a $250,000 fine (See chapter titled, "The Rooter"), the league's owners passed a set of rules loosely referred to as the "Cuban rules of conduct." Among the new stipulations was a ban on owners venturing onto the court during games. During a meeting among league officials and owners regarding the new statutes, Cuban walked out before the vote of the owners. "I was pissed that, of all the things the league needed to pay attention to, this was on the top of their list," he said. "It showed how political the league is. But I'm well past that."[3]

Stern said part of the justification for the rules was to prevent owners from overshadowing the games.

---

[3] Leonard, D. (2007). MARK CUBAN MAY BE A BILLIONAIRE, BUT WHAT HE REALLY NEEDS IS RESPECT. Fortune, 156(8), 172-182.

Therein lies one of many differences between the two adversaries. Cuban's brand is about being in the spotlight. He may not want to completely dominate the game action, but he does want to be a part of it. His anarchistic ways support his personal brand and are part of what makes him a fan favorite. They are also the antithesis of Stern's desire to have law and order in his league, especially amongst the ownership group. He is about structure and control, and part of maintaining control is structuring the league in a way that owners stay in the background.

While the two have had many differences and exchanges of fine payments over the years, Cuban does have respect for Stern as a visionary. When asked about the commissioner's legacy as he prepares to leave the office after 30 years, Cuban replied: "I think it's one of a focus on growth and recognizing that the NBA is in the entertainment business and that it's a global product, not just a local product. Whatever platforms that took us to, he was ready to go. He wasn't protective at all. He was wide open. I think that was great."[4]

Perhaps Cuban and Stern aren't so different after all.

---

[4] Mark Cuban Teases David Stern. ESPN.com, October 26, 2012. Retrieved from http://espn.go.com/dallas/nba/story/_/id/8556905/dallas-mavericks-mark-cuban-jokes-save-money-fines-david-stern-gone

Neither, for that matter, are he and Donald Trump, who has also drawn Cuban's ire on several occasions.

The feud between the two billionaire celebrities began in 2004 when Cuban hosted *The Benefactor*, a short-lived reality-based program in which Cuban would give a $1 million prize to the contestant that demonstrated the skills Cuban deemed necessary to be successful.

Many, including Trump, thought the show was a copy-cat of *The Apprentice*, which had debuted months before. The cancellation of *The Benefactor* prompted Trump to write a slap-in-the-face letter to Cuban. Cuban kept it for almost a decade, then read it aloud during a March 2013 episode of *The Tonight Show* (an earlier appearance than the one in which he criticized Major League Baseball).

Trump's letter read:

> "I am truly sorry to hear that your show has been canceled for lack of ratings. When I initially called you to congratulate you on The Benefactor -- little did you or I realize how disastrous and embarrassing it would turn out to be for you. If you ever decide to do another show, please call me and I will be happy to lend a helping hand."

That fanned the flames of a Twitter war between the two that had been brewing for several months. In November 2012, Cuban offered Trump $1 million to shave his head shortly after the latter publicly offered President Barack Obama $5 million to produce a birth certificate that would prove he's an American citizen.

Following Cuban's *Tonight Show* jab, Trump responded with a series of tweets critical of his rival, 17 in less than a week, including:

> "**@mcuban** has less TV persona than any other person I can think of. He's an arrogant, crude, dope who met some very stupid people."

> "why does **@mcuban** continue to embarrass the 31-35 & 11th place **@dallasmavs** with childish behavior."

When a follower asked Trump "what's the best confidence builder," Trump responded that it was "going against losers like Mark Cuban!"

Cuban, of course, responded: "You just see this crazy life I have & you're in awe. I'm just gonna take over the world while you getting mad." [5]

Cuban also makes his beefs with former Mavericks players and opposing team members public. In 2012, Cuban thought he had an agreement with veteran point guard Jason Kidd, believing he would retire from the franchise. Instead, Kidd signed a free agent deal with the New York Knicks.

Cuban publicly expressed his discontent over Kidd's decision:

> "I thought he (Kidd) was coming (back). I was pissed. J-Kidd's a big boy, he can do whatever he wants. But you don't change your mind like that. I'm sure I'll get over it at some point, but as of right now, I wouldn't put J-Kidd's number in the rafters." [6]

---

[5] Twitter Wars: Donald Trump vs Mark Cuban. Yahoo.com, March 19, 2013. Retrieved from http://sports.yahoo.com/blogs/nba-ball-dont-lie/twitter-wars-donald-trump-vs-mark-cuban-183542949--nba.html
[6] Mark Cuban Won't Retire Jason Kidd's Jersey Because He Went to the Knicks. Yahoo.com, August 21, 2012. Retrieved from http://sports.yahoo.com/blogs/nba-ball-dont-lie/mark-cuban-won-t-retire-jason-kidd-jersey-223414404--nba.html

One of Cuban's most infamous run-ins with a player occurred in 2009. After a Mavericks game with the Denver Nuggets in Denver, in which Dallas lost on a last-second three-pointer, Cuban reportedly confronted the mother of then-Nuggets forward Kenyon Martin and called her son a "thug" and a "punk." Cuban was reportedly upset about Martin's physical style of play during the game. Cuban later apologized on his blog. [7]

Cuban doesn't limit his sharp tongue to matters of basketball. He is a journalist's dream source in that he will dispense his opinion on just about any topic he follows, without a single thought about filtering himself for political correctness. He doesn't even need to be asked a question; through his blog and Twitter feed, he will volunteer his beliefs. And no matter whether it's his own writing or an article by somebody else, Cuban almost never offers an opinion without a heavy dose of expletives and sarcasm.

Mark Cuban on the stock market: "Wall Street has done an AMAZING job of creating conventional wisdom. 'Buy and Hold' is the 2nd most misleading marketing slogan ever, after the brilliant 'rinse and repeat' message on every shampoo bottle. We as a

---

[7] Report: Cuban called Martin a 'Thug'. ESPN.com, May 11, 2009. Retrieved from http://sports.espn.go.com/nba/playoffs/2009/news/story?id=4157481

country have fallen for it. Every message from every marketer of stocks tell us: Young or old, if you can hold for the long term, things will work out for you. That is total bullshit. It's for suckers." [8]

Mark Cuban on large publicly traded corporations: "I'm not against government involvement in times of need. I am for recognizing that big public companies will continue to cut jobs in an effort to prop up stock prices, which in turn stimulates the need for more government involvement." [9]

Mark Cuban on the merits of earning an MBA degree: "I think an MBA is an absolute waste of money. If you have a hole in your knowledge base, there are a ton of online courses you can take. I don't give any advantage to someone in hiring because they have an MBA." [10]

---

[8] The Stock Market is for Suckers... Blog Maverick, January 3, 2006. Retrieved from
http://blogmaverick.com/2006/01/03/the-stock-market-is-for-suckers/

[9] The Most Patriotic Thing You Can Do. Blog Maverick, September 19, 2011. Retrieved from
http://blogmaverick.com/2011/09/19/the-most-patriotic-thing-you-can-do-2/

[10] Mark Cuban: What Entrepreneurs Need to Know Before Starting a Business. Entrepreneur.com, December 26, 2012. Retrieved from
http://www.entrepreneur.com/blog/225357

Another institution Cuban has expressed contempt for is politics. He rarely makes contributions to political campaigns or organizations, despite having more than enough money to do so. He summed up his sentiments about the way politicians try to fix the economy in a blog post during the 2008 presidential campaign:

"The cure to our economic problems is the Entrepreneurial Spirit of All Americans. Instead of bitching at each other, could one Presidential candidate please show even the least bit of leadership and character and stand up for and encourage the entrepreneurs in this country?

I don't care who is friends with whom, who preached when you went to church, whether you know the actual role of the Vice President, whether you voted with President Bush. I don't care about any of the mudslinging going back and forth. All it does is waste the time of every potential voter. All of that is meaningless.

What we need is our candidates to stop yelling at each other and start looking at the American people and encouraging the best of who we are. That is who I want to get behind.

That is what I would like to see for our country." [11]

Several of Cuban's most recent business ventures revolve around investigative journalism. He started a non-profit foundation that funds three websites designed to expose the malfeasance of government and corporations.

ShareSleuth.com investigates and reports on white collar fraud and other abuses of capitalism, while BailoutSleuth.com "tracks the flow of taxpayer money from the Troubled Asset Relief Program and other federal economic stability initiatives, with an emphasis on transparency and accountability." It also reports on bank failures. The third site, JunketSleuth.com, tracks travel by federal employees, members of Congress and their staffs.

"The websites are because I have a strong distrust for the one percent of government employees who put their careers ahead of doing the right thing," Cuban said. "These efforts were a response to that. If we catch one government crook or provide the information that allows someone else to do so, it will have been worth it. I consider it a small price to pay

---

[11] The Cure to our Economic Problems. Blog Maverick, October 23, 2008. Retrieved from http://blogmaverick.com/2012/09/17/the-cure-to-our-economic-problems-2/

for doing a civic duty. I consider it a patriotic effort. If Share Sleuth continues to discover less-than-savory activity in the business world, it's worth it." [12]

In addition to the websites, his AXS TV network's signature program is *Dan Rather Reports*, which allows the former CBS News anchor to uncover wrongdoing in government and the corporate world. And Cuban's 2929 Productions produced an award winning documentary detailing the Enron scandal, called *The Smartest Guys in the Room*.

Cuban also has contempt for some of his fellow billionaires and upper class citizens who do everything they can to avoid paying taxes and make even more money. He writes that the most patriotic think a person can do is "bust your ass and get rich. Make a boatload of money. Pay your taxes. Lots of taxes. Hire people. Train people. Pay people. Spend money on rent, equipment, services. Pay more taxes. When you make a shitload of money, do something positive with it. If you are smart enough to make it, you will be smart enough to know where to put it to work." [13]

---

[12] Mark Cuban's Business Model. Columbia Journalism Review, February 23, 2011. Retrieved from http://www.cjr.org/reports/mark_cubans_business_model.php?page=all

[13] The Most Patriotic Thing You Can Do. Blog Maverick, September 19, 2011. Retrieved from

Though he doesn't think tax policy prevents people from becoming successful, he has the opposite to say about the U.S. patent system. But he didn't just write a blog or talk about his disdain for the system on a talk show. In true Cuban fashion, the bombastic billionaire funded an endowed chair at The Electronic Frontier Foundation, a digital civil rights organization. He titled the chair, "The Mark Cuban Chair to Eliminate Stupid Patents."

His issue with the current system: "Dumbass patents are crushing small businesses. I have had multiple small companies I am an investor in have to fight or pay trolls for patents that were patently ridiculous. There is no place for software patents and most tech patents are not original in the first place. They are merely 'remixes' of early technology." [14]

Another institution he would like to dismantle is the NCAA, the governing body of collegiate sports. Cuban was once quoted as saying he wants to buy

---

http://blogmaverick.com/2011/09/19/the-most-patriotic-thing-you-can-do-2/

[14] Mark Cuban's Awesome Justification for Endowing a Chair to 'Eliminate Stupid Patents.' Techcrunch.com, January 31, 2013. Retrieved from http://techcrunch.com/2013/01/31/mark-cubans-awesome-justification-for-endowing-a-chair-for-eliminating-stupid-patents/

four colleges and extract them from the authority of the NCAA. The reason: he thinks college athletes should be paid, and he would personally pay for scholarships and for their services as athletes.

> "If you're in the Journalism School and you get a job working for The Wall Street Journal during spring semester, and you get paid for it, that wouldn't be a bad thing. That would be a grand slam. That would be something everyone would be proud of... And it's the same with everything except athletics... the NCAA doesn't want you to be the best athlete. They want you to be the best amateur athlete.

> So to me, that's just hypocrisy. I can't do it while I own an NBA team. But if I could pull that off, it would be one of the few reasons I would sell the Mavs. Just to be able to shove it up the NCAA's rear..." [15]

Being a maverick is about more than challenging authority and the status quo. Mark Cuban, the maverick, establishes the foundation for his many other identities.

---

[15] 20 Questions for Mark Cuban. Magbloom.com, February/March 2008. Retrieved from http://www.magbloom.com/wp-content/uploads/2012/02/20Q_bloom10.pdf

He is also an architect who has built empires based on his ideas, his drive, and his determination.

He is a visionary who spots the potential of new technology long before the masses.

He is an entertainer who brings unique content to his TV network and movie theater chain.

He is a rooter of all sports, the ultimate fan who will never shed that fandom for the sake of team ownership.

He is an investor who has maximized his wealth and helped others off the ground.

He is a celebrity who never shies from a camera or a spotlight.

And he is a king, not in the royal sense, but in his own world.

His kingdom began in a modest Pittsburgh neighborhood with a stack of garbage bags and a desire for some new shoes.

Chapter 2: The Architect

At the age of 12, Mark Cuban wanted something.

What he desired was a new pair of shoes, Pumas to be exact. His father, while playing cards with his friends, refused. The ones Mark already had were adequate, his father reasoned, adding that he would not provide his son with anything more than his basic needs.

If the young boy wanted more, he would have to earn it.

Cuban learned for the first time that nobody was just going to hand him money or possessions.

During this encounter, one of his father's card-playing buddies jokingly suggested he earn extra money by selling garbage bags in the neighborhood door-to-door. Young Mark Cuban took him seriously, figuring every house needed garbage bags.

He earned enough for his Pumas.

Cuban was born to sell. Once, as a youngster, he accompanied his father to a large stamp collecting show. He bought several stamps on one floor, then turned right around and sold them -- at the same show -- for a profit on another floor. [16]

Nobody gave Mark money for college, so he earned it by selling stamps and coins, starting a chain letter, and giving paid disco lessons. He also, while still in school, managed to purchase a bar near the University of Indiana. To accomplish this he raised money, selling shares of this business to his friends. He lured customers in the door with cheap drinks and wet T-shirt contests, then schmoozed them enough that, as one acquaintance put it: "People came to see him." [17]

In his early career after college, Cuban discovered that jobs came with strings attached. It wasn't just the trade-off between doing a certain amount of work for a certain amount of pay. He discovered quickly that the employee-employer relationship offered little freedom. Back in those days, few of his supervisors would give him the space or the permission to showcase the full breadth of his skills and hard work.

---

[16] Mark Cuban: From Neighborhood VAR to Internet Czar. CRN.com, October 22, 1999. Retrieved from http://www.crn.com/news/channel-programs/18810686/mark-cuban-from-neighborhood-var-to-internet-czar.htm

[17] Leonard, D. (2007). MARK CUBAN MAY BE A BILLIONAIRE, BUT WHAT HE REALLY NEEDS IS RESPECT. Fortune, 156(8), 172-182.

They tried to put Cuban in a box. And when they did, he broke free.

His first escape occurred during his initial job out of college, at Mellon Bank in his hometown of Pittsburgh. Cuban earned a job helping to computerize the bank's electronic files. While many college grads would have been satisfied just having a job during a period of economic recession in 1980, Cuban wanted to be more entrepreneurial. So he sent notes to the CEO with cut-out magazine articles about how the company could save money. He started a group called the Rookie Club made up of the bank's younger employees and would invite senior executives to talk to the bunch. He started a company newsletter.

All of these efforts failed to earn Cuban the praise from his boss he thought he had earned. He received the exact opposite. One day, his supervisor called Cuban into the office and asked him "Who the f--- do you think you are?" When Cuban defended his actions, the boss told him never to go over him again. Cuban left the company shortly after.

He made his way back to Indiana for a brief time before his college friends coaxed him to move to Dallas. They promised abundant jobs and women.

He got a position as a salesperson for Your Business Software, which sold PC software to businesses and consumers, and quickly rose to be one of its top salesman. This was largely due to the hands-on technical skills he developed by reading manuals and studying computer code.

One day, he was scheduled to open up the office, but instead wanted to close a sale with a customer and collect a $15,000 check, a tenth of which Cuban would receive as commission. His boss told him no, but Cuban disobeyed and picked up the check.

He was fired on the spot.

"But being fired from that job was the determining factor in my business life," Cuban wrote. "I decided then and there to start my own company. I didn't have that much to lose, and it was something that I knew I had to do." [18]

What he did have was a Rolodex full of contacts. Working from his apartment, he called those former clients and offered to service their computers with a money-back guarantee. In 1983, he started a company called MicroSolutions using a $500 loan from a client of his sales gig. The company sold

---

[18] Burke, M. (2013). At Age 25 Mark Cuban Learned Lessons About Leadership That Changed His Life. Forbes.Com

software, and also provided training and software configuration.

Cuban wrote his own programs and immersed himself in the industry by studying Microsoft and Lotus. He eventually transitioned the company into developing local area networks, which is when things really took off.

Following their leader, MicroSolutions's employees worked long hours. Cuban offered competitive prices but a level of customer service typically provided only by high-end providers. He studied every new technology that came on the market to an obsessive degree, to ensure he knew more about it than anybody. He became a beta tester and proving ground for innovation.

But technical knowledge was only part of the equation to building a successful enterprise. Cuban understood the power of a strong brand image. While similar companies housed themselves in humble accommodations to limit their overhead expenses, Cuban rented space in the Dallas Infomart, the Taj Mahal of Dallas' high-tech industry. Apple, MCI WorldCom and Xerox had offices there, and Cuban wanted MicroSolutions to appear just as big. [19]

---

[19] Mark Cuban: From Neighborhood VAR to Internet Czar. CRN.com, October 22, 1999. Retrieved from

Cuban read business books and pored over market research as much as computer manuals. The knowledge he acquired kept him one step ahead of his competitors. His competitive spirit drove him to increase that gap. His salesmanship got him invited to industry events reserved for big players, and also helped him find partners to subsidize his rent and marketing initiatives.

Another key to the success of MicroSolutions was its disproportionately high number of salespeople compared to rivals. Cuban wanted more feet on the street so the company could make more calls, knock on more doors and always be ready to respond when opportunity arose.

By the time he sold the firm in 1990 to CompuServe, MicroSolutions was generating $30 million in revenues and employed 85 people.

"I ended up making about $2.2 million," Cuban said. "I bought a lifetime pass on American Airlines and I just started traveling."

http://www.crn.com/news/channel-programs/18810686/mark-cuban-from-neighborhood-var-to-internet-czar.htm

After "retiring" for a few years, the lure of business and competition were too much. Cuban and his college friend Todd Wagner founded AudioNet, which later became Broadcast.com.

Cuban has been interviewed countless times, but anybody who reads his blog posts or approaches the man himself hoping for some instantaneous magic potion for prosperity will be sorely disappointed. Every piece of advice he's ever given boils down to a concept that is simple to explain, but hard for many to execute: Entrepreneurs just have to take the chance and work hard to make it happen.

In his book, *How to Win at the Sport of Business*, Cuban lays out 12 rules for entrepreneurs. The first one is "Don't start a company unless it's an obsession." The second rule is that having an exit strategy demonstrates that your pursuit is not an obsession. In his view, if a business is an obsession, it's not really a risk to go after it because being obsessed means doing all the necessary preparation and leg work to make the company grow. An entrepreneur's obsession means he or she can persuade prospects and make sales, even if they say no a few times.

One of Cuban's favorite expressions is "No Balls, No Baby." He taught this lesson to a friend during the startup phase of MicroSolutions. Cuban and the acquaintance were walking together when Cuban asked him to become a partner in his new business. The friend hemmed and hawed before finally passing on the opportunity. Cuban slapped the man in the face. When asked why, Cuban responded: "That's your wake-up call in life, pal. When opportunity presents itself, you need to be prepared to take it." Cuban never asked again.[20]

> "Most people don't want to cross that line. There's safety on one side, uncertainty on the other. Most people don't take that step. And it's not even so much that they're afraid to take the step; it's that they know deep down that they didn't do the work necessary to be prepared, and that's the big difference. Most people think, 'Oh, I have a great idea, and the only thing missing is that I don't have the connections, I don't have the access to money.' But that's the biggest bunch of bullshit. The minute anyone says that to me, I know they're a failure.
>
> Because if you're prepared and you know what it takes, it's not a risk. You just have to

figure out how to get there. There is always a way to get there." [21]

Another one of Cuban's strongly held beliefs is that entrepreneurs should never finance their startups with debt. "There are so many uncertainties involved with starting a business, yet the one certainty that you have is paying back your loan. And the bank doesn't care about your business." [22]

So how does a company get started? Again, it's about effort. Especially in today's world, capital is not necessary for the large majority of startup companies, he says. Studying some of Cuban's philosophies and reading what his business acquaintances say about him reveals several themes.

First, Cuban believes business owners need to do the work themselves when they're starting out. Entrepreneurs make the mistake of spending too much on things they could do themselves, either because they don't want to work hard enough or

---

[21] What I've Learned: Mark Cuban. Esquire.com, November 17, 2008. Retrieved from http://www.esquire.com/features/what-ive-learned/ESQ1206BBCUBAN_182_1
[22] MARK CUBAN, O. (n.d). MARK CUBAN, OWNER, DALLAS MAVERICKS IS INTERVIEWED ON BLOOMBERG TV REGARDING ENTREPRENEURS. Financial Markets Regulatory Wire, June 13, 2013

because they think too big to begin with. Do your own advertising instead of hiring a marketing firm. Make your own sales calls rather than hiring salespeople. And use your own money instead of borrowing from a bank. As you grow and start to earn money, then you can use those profits to reinvest in your business.

Even as large as it has grown, Cuban believes in keeping his empire as flat as possible. "If you have managers reporting to managers in a startup, you will fail," he wrote in his book. "Once you get beyond startup, if you have managers reporting to managers, you will create politics."

A man who hands out free game systems to his players and free ice cream bars to his office staff nonetheless despises the idea of smaller companies and startups spending on unnecessary items. "A sure sign of failure for a startup is when someone sends me logo-embroidered polo shirts," he writes in the book. "If your people are at shows and in public, it's okay to buy for your own employees, but if you really think people are going to wear your branded polo when they're out and about, you are mistaken and have no idea how to spend your money."

His other rules are fairly simple. Hire people who will love working for you and make sure they're having fun on the job. Know exactly how your company will make sales. Work on building a company, not an empire. "If the person demands to fly first class or to bring over a personal secretary, run away. If an exec won't go on sales calls, run away. They are empire builders and will pollute your company."

He also believes that you can't rely on your customers to tell you want they want. It's your job as the entrepreneur to convince them they want what you're offering.

"Entrepreneurs need to be reminded that it's not the job of their customers to know what they don't. In other words, your customers have a tough enough time doing their jobs. They don't spend time trying to reinvent their industries or how their jobs are performed. Sure, every now and then you come across an exception. But you can't bet the company on your finding that person among your customers.

Instead, part of every entrepreneur's job is to invent the future. I also call it 'kicking your own ass.' Someone is out there looking to put you out of business. Someone is out there who thinks they have a better idea than you have. A better solution than you have. A better or more efficient product than you have. If there is someone out there who can 'kick your ass' by doing it better, it's part of your job as the owner of the company to stay ahead of them and 'kick your own ass' before someone else does." [23]

Cuban's love of sports played a part in his entrepreneurial success. He loves to compete and considers business the ultimate sport, whether he's a player or coaching a startup in which he's invested.

As a student at Indiana University, Cuban participated on the school's rugby team. When recently asked about the lessons he learned from the rugged, violent sport that carried over into his business life, Cuban replied: "When it hurts, keep on going. That you can always play a little harder. That there's going to be someone bigger and faster and stronger all the time, and hopefully you can play a little bit smarter. And teamwork counts. When you're in a scrum or in a pack, not always the biggest guys push the scrum the farthest. And not always the biggest guys tackle the hardest. You learn what teamwork means and how to push yourself personally." [24]

---

[23] Mark Cuban on Why You Should Never Listen to Your Customers. Entrepreneur.com, December 20, 2011. Retrieved from http://www.entrepreneur.com/article/222501
[24] 20 Questions for Mark Cuban. Magbloom.com, February/March 2008. Retrieved from

Translation: Cuban doesn't believe any excuse exists for a passionate, hard-working entrepreneur to not succeed in business. Competition doesn't matter. The regulatory environment doesn't matter. Tax laws don't matter. The political climate doesn't matter. Your education doesn't matter. The state of the economy doesn't matter.

In fact, Cuban had to overcome a major crisis in the early days of MicroSolutions. An employee of the company embezzled $83,000 of the $85,000 the company had in the bank. Cuban started counting the months that MicroSolutions had been open, hoping it would last. He proudly boasts that after the theft, the company never had a month in which it lost money. [25]

Cuban not only believes that entrepreneurship is the key to his fulfillment, he also contends that it's the key to economic recovery in the U.S.

> "It's always the new idea that re-energizes this country. Industry, manufacturing, transportation, technology, digital

http://www.magbloom.com/wp-content/uploads/2012/02/20Q_bloom10.pdf

[25] Mark Cuban, Billionaire. (Scared, Broke and Jobless). Subvertmagazine.com, September 10, 2012. Retrieved from http://www.subvertmagazine.com/blog/mark-cuban/

communications, etc., each changed how we lived and ignited our economy and standard of living. Tax policy has never done that. The American People have." [26]

"Entrepreneurs don't think about current economic times before they start a business. They think about the validity of their idea, the opportunity it affords them, and what it will take to be successful. If anything, many people will find themselves on the unfortunate side of job cuts and use it as motivation and a catalyst to start a business. I happen to believe that when your back is up against the wall, you will work harder and smarter to make your dreams come true." [27]

---

[26] The Cure to Our Economic Problems. Blog Maverick, October 23, 2008. Retrieved from http://blogmaverick.com/2012/09/17/the-cure-to-our-economic-problems-2/

[27] The Cure to Our Economic Problems. Blog Maverick, October 23, 2008. Retrieved from http://blogmaverick.com/2012/09/17/the-cure-to-our-economic-problems-2/

Chapter 3: The Visionary

In 1994, the World Wide Web was still a vast unknown. A select few had figured out how to market and advertise on the Internet, and fewer still had ascertained its potential as an entirely new business model and distribution channel.

By the middle of the year, there were less than 2,500 total websites in operation.

WhiteHouse.gov had just launched, as did a search engine known as Yahoo (the exclamation point hadn't appeared yet). America Online beckoned people to the new, exciting world of the Internet by sending sample CDs in the mail. At the time, there was no Google or eBay. Facebook was still over a decade away.

The late 90's mania surrounding Internet stocks was still on the horizon.

Most companies didn't have their own websites yet, nor did they provide widespread access to their office minions. The early adopters of the Internet logged on through their phone line, meaning that a website containing anything beyond basic text might take several minutes to load.

And yet, in 1994, college friends and soon-to-be lifelong business partners Todd Wagner and Mark Cuban predicted the Internet would evolve from offering just static text to providing real-time audio and video. This was 11 years before the debut of YouTube, which only allowed people to watch recorded video. Someday, they believed, people would look to their computers for live entertainment and sports programming instead of their televisions.

Their prediction came true, in part, because they followed one of Cuban's edicts for entrepreneurship. Quoting from technology luminary Alan Kay, Cuban believes: "The best way to predict the future is to invent it." [28]

According to accounts, Wagner pitched the idea of AudioNet to Cuban: Bringing live sporting events to the Internet so that people could listen to the games they wanted to. It would be a revolution, allowing fans to follow their teams anywhere in the world, so long as they had an Internet connection.

As savvy entrepreneurs, they did what many web companies failed to do... fill a real consumer need.

---

[28] Mark Cuban on Why You Should Never Listen to Your Customers. Entrepreneur.com, December 20, 2011. Retrieved from http://www.entrepreneur.com/article/222501

After all, did anybody really want to buy dog food over the Internet?

Specifically, the two men addressed one of their own needs. They wanted to follow the games of their alma mater, Indiana University. But one was hard-pressed at the time to find a Hoosier basketball game on in the Dallas market, unless ESPN or another network broadcast it nationally.

With such a mobile society, thousands of sports fans were now living far away from the teams they grew up with or supported in college. Prior to their company, Cuban and Wagner's only recourse was to call a friend who had access to an Indiana radio broadcast and have that person hold the phone up to the radio.

AudioNet was born in 1995, with a $5,000 investment, and the partners set up shop in a spare bedroom in Cuban's house. They purchased a Packard Bell PC, networking equipment and a high-speed Internet connection.

Soon they had persuaded a Dallas radio station to allow them to record broadcasts, which Cuban and Wagner would digitize and post on their website. A few months later they brought live broadcasts to the site by hooking up a radio tuner to the sound card in the computer.

Cuban explained during a 1999 interview with *VideoMaker Magazine* that the mission of his and Wagner's company was to turn the Internet into a broadcast medium. "We have put together the technology, infrastructure and software, and have aggregated content in order to aggregate audience. With this base, we offer content creators the ability to put their products of all kinds in front of an audience at a minimal cost." [29]

Interest quickly grew. Cuban and Wagner gave a 5 percent stake to Host Communications, which had the broadcast rights to 12 NCAA basketball teams and the NCAA men's basketball tournament, also known as March Madness. Then, they managed to sign exclusive agreements with most major colleges and universities and the National Football League, which allowed them to live stream the Super Bowl.

AudioNet soon expanded beyond sports and news broadcasts into business services, when they provided Internet broadcasting of conference calls, investor conferences, stockholder meetings and training sessions. At its peak, the company had deals with over 300 radio stations, 40 television stations, 400 sports teams, and 600 business customers.

---

[29] The Future of Video on the Internet. Blog Maverick, June 7, 2012. Retrieved from http://blogmaverick.com/2012/06/07/the-future-of-video-on-the-internet/

Despite its popularity, the company could not turn a profit. After spending a few million dollars of their own money, the partners sold shares in $30,000 increments to local investors and friends. Then they received another capital infusion through a private placement.

In 1998, the company was renamed Broadcast.com and went public with the goal of becoming the top broadcasting portal on the Internet. At the time of its IPO, Broadcast.com had fewer than $7 million in revenues, $28 million in equity, and an accumulated debt of nearly $10 million. The company had little to no chance of achieving profitability in the foreseeable future.

Of course, it was 1998. So a lack of profitability didn't stop enthusiastic investors from boosting the stock's value 249 percent on its first day of trading.

With more capital, Cuban and Wagner continued to expand the business. They purchased a company called Net Roadshow, which broadcast the roadshows that companies embarked upon when they were preparing for their initial public offerings.

Broadcast.com established a joint venture with a Japanese company to provide content in that language. Then it entered into a licensing agreement with Trimark Holdings to broadcast the company's entire film library. The company nearly crashed the Internet in February 1999 when Broadcast.com attracted 1.5 million viewers to watch a live Victoria's Secret fashion show.

The racy stunt helped put their website on the map.

How far ahead could Cuban think? In the aforementioned interview with VideoMaker in 1999, he essentially foretold the creation of YouTube, which would occur six years later. He said that it wouldn't be long until most of the streaming video on the Internet will be homemade videos.

"It will be so easy to present video to small audiences. Instead of the summer vacation or wedding video sitting on the shelf, we will post them on our family web sites so that grandma and grandpa can watch whenever they want. We will do the same with high schools posting their games, debates and school plays. It will be far more convenient than corralling everyone into the family room or making copies of the tape to send everywhere." [30]

---

[30] The Future of Video on the Internet. Blog Maverick, June 7, 2012. Retrieved from http://blogmaverick.com/2012/06/07/the-future-of-video-on-the-internet/

But the company itself may have been too far ahead of its time. Even with all its efforts, Broadcast.com couldn't get in the black. Its operating loss for 1998 was $15 million. So when Yahoo! approached Wagner and Cuban about acquiring the firm in April 1999, they spent little time debating the decision before agreeing to take the deal.

Competitors like Microsoft and America Online had moved in. Yahoo! was desperate to add Broadcast.com's capabilities to maintain its title as the leading web portal.

Yahoo! needed to upgrade from its regular text-only content to the multimedia capabilities that Broadcast.com offered. They purchased Cuban's and Wagner's brainchild for more than $5 billion.

Mark Cuban was officially a billionaire.

The duo joined the likes of Jeff Bezos, founder of Amazon.com, and others who invested in the potential of the Internet before most people recognized it. Yet, unlike many of those pioneers, Cuban and Wagner also recognized that the mania surrounding the Internet sector was not sustainable.

By February 2000, despite the fact that few of these companies had ever turned a simple profit, the market capitalization of Internet stocks accounted for 6 percent of the total market cap for all U.S. public companies. In two years, the entire sector had earned more 1000 percent returns. Part of the reason for the run-up was the rampant buying and selling of these stocks; about 20 percent of all publicly traded volume over this period was speculation in Internet stocks.[31] The demand for these issues continued to push share prices higher and higher.

Cuban and Wagner knew, like with anything in business, values can only go so high so fast before the bubble pops. Unable to turn a profit on Broadcast.com and with a sweet offer for the still unprofitable firm, the partners got out. And in keeping with their concern that Internet stocks were greatly overvalued, they hedged the Yahoo! stock used to make the acquisition and didn't lose the value of their shares when the acquiring company's stock tanked with the rest of the market. Had they not, the story of Mark Cuban would be a lot different today.

Cuban considers himself lucky. He also believes he created much of that luck on his own. He can see the future largely because he creates it -- at least in his corner of the universe. He doesn't jump on bandwagons; he launches them. He can study a new

---

[31] Dotcom Mania: The Rise and Fall of Internet Stock Prices. Eli Ofek and Matthew Richardson, National Bureau of Economic Research. December 2001. Retrieved from http://www.nber.org/papers/w8630.pdf?new_window=1

technology or emerging trend and visualize it five or 10 years down the road.

So if Mark Cuban were explaining the accomplishments of Broadcast.com, he wouldn't attribute the success to being ahead of the game. He would likely brag that the duo created a game that people, once they discovered it, wanted to play. And had this been the only time that Cuban invented a prosperous future, one could write it off as luck or good timing. But he did it again seven years later.

A blogger named James Altucher was contacted by Broadcast.com in 1997. At the time, Altucher ran a company called Reset, which was putting together the first regular live online production of a TV show, *The People's Court*. Broadcast.com wanted to use Reset's technology to do live streaming. Altucher later wrote about the interaction in a blog post titled "How I Helped Mark Cuban Make a Billion Dollars and the 5 Things I Learned from Him."

What he learned speaks to Cuban's visionary prowess:

> "Most people I speak to about Cuban say he was lucky. He created a company with minimal revenues in the internet video/audio space, had the biggest IPO in history at the time (1998), immediately put the company up for sale, sold to the biggest Internet

company (Yahoo!), and then sold all his shares at the very top. How did he know to sell at the top? Is that the 'luck' part everyone refers to? Or the fact that he started a company with no revs and was just 'lucky' it was at the right time (the Internet bubble?)

It wasn't luck at all. In chess there's a saying, 'only the good players are lucky.' Whenever a good player wins a game, the angry opponent often says, 'ahh, you were just lucky.' But it always seems the good player gets lucky more than the bad player.

He knew, probably five years in advance, that a bubble was occurring and this was the exact plan to maximize value from it. He probably extracted more from the initial Internet bubble than anyone else. It doesn't happen by luck that you sell at the top. You have to know five years in advance when that top will occur. And then have to have a very precise plan for being at the right spot at the right time at the very top." [32]

---

[32] How I Helped Mark Cuban Make a Billion Dollars and 5 Things I Learned from Him. The Altucher Confidential. Retrieved from http://www.jamesaltucher.com/2011/04/why-im-jealous-of-mark-cuban-and-5-things-i-learned-from-him/

Cuban splurged on himself after collecting his payday from the sale of Broadcast.com. One of his acquisitions was a high-definition TV with a 100-inch projection screen. It cost him around $10,000. Just like with the Internet in 1994, HDTV in 2000 was still a novelty. In fact, Cuban recalls that only one channel on his new DirectTV package offered high-definition programming. It consisted of a continuous loop of about 90 minutes worth of animal footage and old sports reels.

Nobody was producing content because few believed that people would pony up for expensive TV sets just because they delivered high-quality pictures. It began as the classic chicken-and-egg scenario: Content providers needed consumers to adopt HDTV before they would invest in content, but consumers weren't going to buy sets without any content available.

That's when Cuban decided to launch the future of HDTV, instead of waiting for it to materialize. He had seen personal computers become affordable in his lifetime, so why wouldn't HDTV sets?

"And if the traditional media couldn't see that — well, it just opened the door for me," Cuban said of the coming HDTV revolution. [33]

---

[33] Heilemann, J. (2004). Mark Cuban's End Game. Business 2.0, 5(11), 46.

He teamed with veteran TV producer Philip Garvin and developed a new network: HDNet on satellite provider DirectTV, which launched in September 2001, just five days before the 9/11 terrorist attacks.

All of the network's original programming was produced in high definition. And though it didn't offer the breadth of programming one could find on the non-high-definition stations, it also bore no resemblance to that running loop he discovered on his satellite package. Months after HDNet launched, it aired exclusive hi-definition coverage of the U.S. invasion of Afghanistan. The following February, the network brought viewers high-definition video of the 2002 Winter Olympics in Salt Lake City.

Its regular programming included space shuttle launches, travel shows, news programs, and male-oriented shows featuring young women in bikinis.

Over the years to come, HDNet would broadcast National Hockey League games, Major League Soccer, auto racing, mixed-martial arts fights, lower-level professional wrestling and the upstart United Football League, which Cuban initially thought about investing in before backing out. Syndicated reruns of cult TV shows filled out the schedule.

Within three years, Cuban had invested more than $100 million into the network. That bought 1,200 hours of original programming filmed in high definition and a robust library of licensed content. The network employed eight crews shooting HD video around the globe, helping to fill the 24/7 network with 15 hours of new, original programming each week.

As his network was growing, so was the industry. Prices for sets were dropping, just as Cuban predicted. In 2002, consumers bought 2.5 million HDTV sets, and another 4 million in 2003. [34]

Cuban later added a second HD network: HDNet Movies, which brought high-definition, commercial-free films to subscribers. The network showed older films that it has transferred in 1080i high definition or shot originally in the format. Many films shown on HDNet Movies had never before been released in HD on other networks.

Of course, high-definition TV is no longer a novelty. HD sets are now about all one can buy, and HD programming has become the rule, not the exception. This evolution has forced Cuban to rebrand his network and position it in a much different way.

---

[34] Gallagher, L. (2004). The Big Picture. (cover story). Forbes, 173(4), 78-82.

Recently renamed AXS TV, the network is now cast as a provider of live television, covering sports (primarily Mixed Martial Arts), pop culture, music, fashion, and other areas. One of its feature programs is still *Dan Rather Reports*, an investigative news magazine nominated for an Emmy award for Outstanding Investigative Journalism.

HDNet was the foundation for a much larger vision Cuban and Wagner would develop during the first decade of the new millennium. The partners have since created a vertically integrated media and entertainment empire with individual properties that represent each aspect of the entertainment supply chain.

Their new company, **2929 Entertainment**, can develop, produce and distribute TV and film programming. The firm owns film distributor Magnolia Pictures, Landmark Theaters and the AXS TV cable networks, among other properties.

With the pieces in place, Cuban and Wagner have sought to create history again, this time by changing all the rules of established media: how it's distributed, how it's marketed and how it's promoted. And in their quest, they are encountering critics who think their ideas will fail, protectionists who want them to fail because it could ruin old business models, and those who anxiously await the new world Cuban envisions.

If there's a lesson would-be entrepreneurs could learn from Cuban's visionary ways, it's this: Success is never about the idea itself. It's about the hard work you perform to take the idea from vision to reality.

"Over the last 20 years, I've always been about what's new, what's next and how am I getting there first. It's a sprint and I have to keep on running 150 miles per hour. It's an adventure." [35]

"Everyone has ideas," Cuban has said. "The hard part is doing the homework to know if the idea could work in an industry, then doing the preparation to be able to execute on the idea. Otherwise, someone who knows more and works harder will kick your ass."

For Mark Cuban, execution is everything.

---

[35] Mark Cuban profile. Business Innovation Factory. Retrieved from http://businessinnovationfactory.com/iss/innovators/mark-cuban

Chapter 4: The Entertainer

Few industries have evolved as rapidly, and have as much uncertainty, as the media business.

It's this rampant fluidity that makes media the perfect haven for an opportunistic, visionary entrepreneur who is driven to succeed but can afford to fail. A person like Mark Cuban.

Consider the developments in mass media over the last 30 years. For the better part of the 20th century, consumers essentially had four options for media consumption.

The print world, including books, magazines, and newspapers, owned a mass media monopoly for generations. Then, recorded music and radio industries took share in the first decades of the century, but not until the 1920s did technological advancements make them more commercially viable. Broadcast television took off in the late 1940s and early 1950s. For the next 30 years, these mediums were about the only options for people to receive information and enjoy content in their homes.

In the late 1970s and early 1980s, the media world began its fragmentation and things would never be the same for consumers. Pay-TV, including basic cable, satellite TV, and subscription channels like HBO, gave viewers more options. Networks like ESPN, CNN, and MTV provided specific niche programming for targeted audiences, a trend that would only get more pronounced as bandwidth opened up and more networks were born.

The Internet opened up an entirely new world beginning in the early 1990s. Much of the content people used to have to pay for suddenly became free. It delivered music and video digitally. It signaled the slow death of physical media, like cassettes, CDs, DVDs and videotapes.

Despite all of these recent advancements, Mark Cuban has the foresight to know that today's devices will soon be obsolete.

> "How many times have we heard someone talk about the future of media and they immediately use their child as an example of what we all will experience in the future?
> Think about your own childhood. Do you still use ANY of the same devices? Still have that cassette player? Still burning those CDs? That Walkman that wowed your parents still wowing anyone? You still carrying your boom box on your shoulder like Radio Raheem? Of course not.

If you think that the tech your young kids are using today is any reflection on what will be used in the future, even in the near future, you are mistaken. It's also short changing the intellect of every kid 18 and under. You don't think they can come up with something better? The reality is that we do not live in the world we were born into. Things change."[36]

Which may explain why Mark Cuban, following the sale of Broadcast.com, has focused more of his energy on content than on distribution. While immersing himself in technology made him a millionaire, selling things that people want to listen to and watch made him a billionaire.

For Mark Cuban, it was back to Hollywood; not in the physical sense, but through a variety of investments in the movie and TV business.

This also meant a reunion with business partner Todd Wagner. The two joined forces to create a vertically integrated entertainment company. But again, Cuban wasn't going to operate his media company like everybody else did.

---

[36] The Dumbest Words in New Media. Blog Maverick, May 10, 2013. Retrieved from http://blogmaverick.com/2013/05/10/the-dumbest-words-in-new-media/

In addition to HDNet, which was renamed **AXS TV** in 2012, and **HDNet Movies**, the partners' company owns: **2929 Productions**, a film production house, **Magnolia Pictures**, a film distributor, and **Landmark Theatres**, a 227-screen theater chain. Each of these companies fits under the umbrella of 2929 Entertainment, and each company represents a unique piece of the movie and TV value and supply chain.

"We realized that because we are vertically integrated, with AXS TV, Landmark Theaters, Magnolia Pictures and 2929 Films, not only could we make, distribute, show and sell movies, but we didn't have to play by all the old Hollywood rules," Cuban said. "I decided to look at the technology opportunities that would allow us to change how the game was played that others may not be aware of." [37]

In the beginning, Cuban struggled to get major cable providers to pony up for HDNet. Some say his antics as an NBA owner had cost him distribution. Several NBA team owners also control cable systems, and the theory went that they refused to carry HDNet because of his intrusion on their fraternity. Others claim it was simply a combination of a lack of

---

[37] Exclusive Conversation with Mark Cuban. The Legacy Series, October 16, 2012.
http://jobslegacy.wordpress.com/tag/innovation/

compelling content and the price Cuban was asking to carry his network. [38]

The same companies that, early on, had refused to carry HDNet turned around and joined forces to create their own high-definition network, called MOJO HD. Many in the industry referred to the network as the "the Cuban killer." [39] But it was MOJO that met its own demise, lasting only 18 months before it was shuttered on December 1, 2008.

Cuban lured the large providers eventually, but they didn't subscribe for long.

As the economy tanked, cable subscribers fled for satellite providers and the cost of premium channels like ESPN skyrocketed, some cable companies cut the cord on HDNet. In May 2009, the network lost access to Time Warner Cable. Later than year, RCN, Mediacom and MetroCast Cablevision stopped carrying the network. In February 2011, HDNet was dropped by Cox.

---

[38] Leonard, D. (2007). MARK CUBAN MAY BE A BILLIONAIRE, BUT WHAT HE REALLY NEEDS IS RESPECT. Fortune, 156(8), 172-182.
[39] Leonard, D. (2007). MARK CUBAN MAY BE A BILLIONAIRE, BUT WHAT HE REALLY NEEDS IS RESPECT. Fortune, 156(8), 172-182.

Several major television providers in Canada also opted not to carry Cuban's network during the same period.

The birth of AXS TV

Now with high-definition TV no longer a novelty, Cuban needed a different hook to attract viewers to his network. With services like Netflix and Hulu, as well as the Internet sites of the major TV and cable networks, recorded programming was quickly migrating from television to the web.

Cuban, ever the visionary, correctly figured this trend would likely continue given the proliferation of tablets and smartphones that allow users to watch recorded programs anywhere they can get an Internet connection. He realized that live programming is the last type of content that is still best delivered on television.

For sports, breaking news and live special events like awards shows and concerts, people will still gravitate to their televisions. What's more, the emergence of social media, especially Twitter, gives viewers an outlet to share their thoughts and opinions with their friends and followers as things unfold.

Live events, Cuban has ascertained, are the only programming left that can draw large simultaneous audiences while helping create buzz via social media.

So in July 2012, Cuban's entertainment company teamed with AEG, Ryan Seacrest Media and Creative Artists Agency to launch AXS TV. The new network replaced HDNet on satellite and cable packages.

AXS TV is branded as the "premier destination for live events, breaking news, and as-they-are-happening trends in the worlds of pop culture, music, fashion, and entertainment."

From multi-day festivals to stadium tours to club acts, AXS TV delivers an unparalleled shared experience for fans of all genres. With multiple live concerts weekly, AXS TV is the number one destination for artists and their fans to experience and share a pure live event in the world of music and pop culture.

"From show creation and development to rehearsals, sound-check and performance and right thru the after-party, AXS TV viewers get an immersive look into their favorite acts touring today from across the globe," read the press release.

The network uses AEG's L.A. LIVE production facilities and has access to the mega-promoter's other worldwide venues.

One example of the network's live music programming is *The World's Greatest Tribute Bands*, a weekly series broadcast live from the Roxy Theatre on Sunset Boulevard in West Hollywood. The show features a different band each week paying tribute to classic artists such as David Bowie, Bon Jovi, Led Zeppelin, Iron Maiden and Pink Floyd.

Live comedy shows from New York's Gotham Comedy Club were also added to the mix.

AXS TV provides some live news content. In April 2013, the network inked a deal with AOL to simulcast several hours of its live web news stream, HuffPost Live. [40]

The movie business

Magnolia Pictures has distributed numerous independent films, including James Marsh's critically acclaimed 2008 documentary *Man on Wire*, about tightrope walker Philippe Petit. The company's home entertainment arm sometimes releases films simultaneously with their theatrical debut via HDNet Movies.

---

[40] AOL's HuffPost Live Gets Shot on Cable with Mark Cuban's AXS TV. Ad Age digital, April 28, 2013. Retrieved from http://adage.com/article/digital/aol-s-huffpost-live-shot-tv-mark-cuban-s-axs-tv/241164/

In 2003, Cuban and Wagner purchased Landmark Theatres from bankruptcy protection. Founded in 1974, Landmark is the largest chain dedicated to showing independent films and its fare skews toward foreign flicks and intellectual avant-garde films. In addition to the initial purchase, Cuban and Wagner spent millions upgrading the chain's facilities.

Today, Landmark operates 227 screens in 50 theaters located in 21 U.S. markets. Many of its theaters are historic landmarks, including the Trivoli in St. Louis, the Inwood in Dallas and the Oriental in Milwaukee.

Cuban's belief in the customer experience shows at a typical Landmark. Movies are digitally projected. The concession stand features gourmet cuisine. Customers can buy DVDs, books and CDs at the theater and several of its facilities feature couches and loveseats. In 2010, the chain introduced environmentally friendly EcoSelect popcorn bags at all of its locations.

With all the pieces of the film creation and distribution channel in place, the company wanted to test a new method of distributing movies. The traditional business model is to release a new film in theaters, followed by a DVD release a few months later, then the movie becomes available on pay-TV movie channels. Cuban and Wagner wanted to test a simultaneous release, giving consumers a choice of how they wanted to see a movie and offering that choice at the same time: in a theater, on DVD, and on HDNet.

They signed up Academy Award-winning director Steven Soderbergh to direct *Bubble*, a murder mystery involving workers in a doll factory located in a struggling small town. Released in February 2006 on a $1.6 million budget, the movie struggled at the box office due to boycotts by theater chains threatened by Cuban's new distribution model. The movie reportedly grossed just $145,000 in its theater run.

Then in 2011, Cuban and Wagner put Landmark and Magnolia up for sale, however they never completed a transaction involving the properties.

"Prices for entertainment properties are up," Cuban said regarding the proposed sale. "If we don't get the price and premium we want, we are happy to continue to make money from the properties."

The company's production house, 2929 Productions, has enjoyed both critical and financial success.

Its biggest achievement was the 2005 release of *Good Night, and Good Luck*, which told the story of the public battle pitting CBS newsmen Edward R. Murrow and Fred Friendly against Wisconsin Senator Joseph McCarthy during the Communism panic of the 1950s. The film featured Jeff Daniels, George Clooney and Robert Downey Jr.

Clooney also directed the film, and *Good Night* earned six Academy Award nominations, including Best Picture, Best Director and Best Original Screenplay. It was also named the Movie of the Year for 2006 by the American Film Institute. Produced for only $7.5 million, the released grossed over $31 million in the U.S. box office.

A year later, the company released another critically acclaimed hit, *Akeelah and the Bee*, about a girl from South Los Angeles trying to qualify for the National Spelling Bee. Its domestic box office gross was nearly $19 million. That same year, 2929 released *The Smartest Guys in the Room*, about the Enron scandal, which earned an Academy Award nomination for Best Documentary.

Cuban and the rest of the production company seem little interested in big budget CGI blockbusters. Among 2929's production credits are *Rejoice and Shout*, a 2010 documentary about the history of Gospel music; *Casino Jack and the United States of Money*, a 2010 investigation into D.C. lobbyist Jack Abramoff; and *Gonzo*, a 2008 documentary detailing the life of famed journalist Hunter S. Thompson.

Look closely at these and other production credits, and a familiar Mark Cuban theme emerges. Celebrate the underdogs and those who champion their cause. Expose the atrocities committed by corrupt institutions. Cuban says the content he provides, be it TV or movies, is just about good business.

> "I'm just looking for programming that I think is going to be memorable, that is going to impact people personally, and stuff that people will think is funny -- kind of like a baby HBO from a content perspective. Most companies, most media companies or public companies, are geared toward earnings per share, and that drives everything: hitting the numbers, hitting the quarter mark...Everybody else does nothing more creative than following the trend. It's like: Let's do another poker show. Now let's extend that to blackjack. Now let's mix blackjack with poker. Now let's pimp my ride, let's pimp my house, let's get tattoos, let's get bounty hunters. If everybody else is doing it, I don't want to do it. Rather than trying to grovel for an extra share of viewers like most media companies do these days, I'd rather just

throw it up against the wall and take some chances." [41]

And yet, Cuban has written in the past about how the economics of movie making and marketing consume him. So much so that he issued an open challenge to readers of his blog: Develop a way to convince five million people to see a film in a theater without spending so much on marketing that it barely breaks even during its theatrical release. Cuban wrote that he'd offer a job to the person who could solve the dilemma.

"It's not unusual to spend 8, 10, 12 dollars PER PERSON that goes to a movie in the opening weekend. Shoot, it's not unusual for studios to spend that much per person to get people to go to the theater through a movie's entire run!

How crazy is it to spend more on marketing than the revenue received when they go to the movie? It's double crazy because that revenue is split with the theater. So if a studio spends 12 bucks to get someone to go to the theater,

[41] What I've Learned: Mark Cuban. Esquire.com, November 17, 2008. Retrieved from http://www.esquire.com/features/what-ive-learned/ESQ1206BBCUBAN_182_1

they might only be getting 4 dollars back in return.

You would think that there has to be a better way than spending 1x, 2x, 3x or more times the initial revenue received opening weekend or week? Right?

So if you want a job, and have a great idea on how to market movies in a completely different way, if your idea works for any and all kinds of movies, if it changes the dynamics and the economics of promoting movies, email it or post it. If it's new and unique, I want to hear about it. If it's a different way of doing the same thing you have seen before, it probably won't get you a job, but feel free to try.

So go for it. Come up with a great idea that I want to use and I will come up with a job for you to make that idea happen.[42]

Cuban provided his own potential solution two years later, when he blogged about an idea for giving away movie soundtrack downloads or other digital content

---

[42] The Movie Business Challenge. Blog Maverick, July 23, 2006. Retrieved from http://blogmaverick.com/2006/07/23/the-movie-business-challenge/

with the purchase of a theater ticket. Developing ways to give people more value for their entertainment dollar has always come easily to Mark Cuban, from the early wet t-shirt contests at his college bar to his most publicized venture, as owner (and chief mascot) of the NBA's Dallas Mavericks.

Chapter 5: The Rooter

On an early winter afternoon in 1999, Cuban entertained an assembly of Harvard Business School alumni at the Dallas Petroleum Club. The club was founded in 1934 as a fraternity of oil men. It bills itself as "one of the finest private clubs in the country in which its members, who include oil and gas executives in the industry, business, finance, education, government, medicine, and the arts, cherish the club because of the personal attention and exceptional service they receive once they enter its quarters."

Business casual dress is required at all times, except in the bar, and cell phone usage is prohibited in the main dining and bar area. [43] It doesn't sound like the kind of place Mark Cuban could spend a lot of time in, given his wheeling-dealing ways and penchant for wearing faded blue jeans and T-shirts.

Though it was set up as a speech, the session became more of a storytelling session, with the bankers and lawyers peppering Cuban with questions about things

---

[43]

http://www.thedallaspetroleumclub.com/viewCustomPage.aspx?id=3

they had heard or read about the newest member of the billionaire's club.

One of the attendees brought up Cuban's purchase of a $40 million Gulfstream airplane, a transaction Cuban claims to have conducted via email. Fresh off the sale of Broadcast.com, Cuban had just recently found himself with $2.5 billion in wealth and an appetite to spend it.

"It was one of the three things I wanted. The first was the house," Cuban told the gathering, referring to the 10-bedroom, 24,000-square-foot Dallas mansion he purchased from a subprime mortgage lender that was in financial trouble. He got the house for $15 million. [44]

"The second was the plane."

An eager voice from the crowed piped up: "What's the third?"

"Ah, ah, ah!" Cuban replied. "I'm keeping that private just now." [45]

[44] (2005). MAVERICK MOGUL. Fast Company, (101), 70.
[45] The Billionaire. Esquire.com, April 1, 2000. Retrieved from http://www.esquire.com/features/billionaire-cuban-sound-0400

On January 14, 2000, Mark Cuban became the majority owner of the Dallas Mavericks of the National Basketball Association, buying the team for $280 million. Cuban wasn't the first fan to buy a team just because he could. But whereas many newbie sports owners struggle to adjust to the different business model of professional athletics, Cuban had the opposite experience.

Prior to Mark Cuban's ownership, the Mavericks were one of the worst franchises in the NBA. Launched in 1980 after millionaire Donald Carter secured the franchise, the Mavericks ended a seven-year absence of professional basketball in Dallas.

From 1967 to 1973, the Dallas Chaparrals played in the American Basketball Association, eventually moving to San Antonio to join the NBA and become the Spurs. The Mavericks began play in the brand new Reunion Arena and quickly became a marginally successful franchise by qualifying for the playoffs six times during the 1980s.

But the 1990s were a different story. They suffered nine consecutive losing seasons prior to Cuban's purchase. From the 1990-91 season through the 1998-99 campaign, the Mavericks won just 28 percent of their games, the worst record of any team in any professional sport during that period. In two seasons combined, from 1992 to 1994, the team won 24 games in TOTAL, while losing 140.

Cuban seemed to make an immediate impact. The team started the 1999-2000 season much the same as recent years, with a record of 9-23 when Cuban took over. The Mavericks quickly rebounded and finished the season 31-19, including 9-1 in the month of April to finish the overall season at 40-42, their best record in 10 years. Although the team missed the playoffs, the foundation was set for a bright future.

Right out of the gate, Cuban sought to improve the climate of the organization. He upgraded the players' hotel and travel accommodations on the road, replaced the bench chairs with more plush models and equipped each team member's locker-room cubicle with a personal stereo, flat-screen monitor, DVD player and Sony PlayStation. He hired eight assistant coaches, about double the normal staff size in the NBA. He paid attention to the morale of the team's office workers, providing them free soft drinks, ice cream bars and massages. Even the little details he addressed, such as replacing the cheap NBA standard towels in the locker room with ones that cost $20 each. [46]

---

[46] Hoffer, R. (2011). NEW DIRECTIONS. Sports Illustrated, 66.

The quick turnaround and his fresh perspective endeared Cuban to long-suffering Mavericks fans. In their eyes, he was spending the kind of money necessary to field a better team on the court. He continued to cheer from the same seats he had in years past, showcasing his energy and enthusiasm for the team. He would regularly shell out $2,000 for after-game drinks at the arena bar when the team won. He reportedly handed out free tickets to attractive women to improve the atmosphere as well.

Cuban engaged with fans personally by encouraging them to email him. He has responded to thousands of those messages, and would often ask fans whether they received good service from the arena ushers and concession workers.

The next season the club finished 53-29 en route to its first playoff appearance in 11 years. Next year the Mavericks moved into the American Airlines Center and promptly set a franchise best record at 57-25, including an NBA best road record of 27-14. That record didn't stand long, as the Mavericks won 60 games the next year, 58 in 2004-2005 and 60 again the year after that.

In 2006, Dallas made its first ever trip to the NBA Finals, winning the first two games of the series before losing the next four and surrendering the championship to the Miami Heat. Game 5 was especially tough, as a ballistic Cuban reportedly shouted in Stern's direction that the league was fixed. Though he denied saying that, he was still fined $250,000. Like a true fan, Cuban was devastated by the series loss; he didn't come out of his house for three weeks and he contemplated selling the team. [47]

But the team's success would continue. Dallas set an all-time team best regular season record the following year at 67-15, but stumbled in the first round of the playoffs, losing to the 8th-seeded Golden State Warriors. The Warriors were coached by Don Nelson, who was the Mavericks' coach when Cuban bought the team. Their relationship started out well, but deteriorated beginning in the 2003 playoffs when Cuban questioned Nelson's reluctance to play an injured Dirk Nowitzki, the squad's top player. It continued during Nelson's contract negotiations. Nelson agreed to coach the team for three seasons, then work for the team as a consultant. That agreement was never fulfilled, and Nelson took the job with Golden State. He later successfully sued Cuban for $6 million in back pay. Cuban the fan took center stage following the playoff loss to the Warriors, accusing his former coach of using

---

[47] Leonard, D. (2007). MARK CUBAN MAY BE A BILLIONAIRE, BUT WHAT HE REALLY NEEDS IS RESPECT. Fortune, 156(8), 172-182.

information he gleaned from his time with the Mavericks to pull off the upset. [48]

The Mavericks looked to have a strong team heading into the 2010-2011 season, its 31st as a franchise. But while making the playoffs seemed like a foregone conclusion, the depth of the league's top contenders would make it an uphill climb to earn that elusive first championship. The Kobe Bryant-led Los Angeles Lakers were the two-time defending champs. The San Antonio Spurs had arguably the most consistently proficient organization in the league, and the upstart Oklahoma City Thunder boasted the best young player in the game, Kevin Durant. In the Eastern Conference, LeBron James, considered the best player in the league, joined the Miami Heat along with Chris Bosh to team up with perennial all-start Dwayne Wade. Many considered "The Big Three" the odds-on favorite to win the title.

Led by Nowitzki, Shawn Marion, Tyson Chandler and Jason Kidd, the Mavericks finished the regular season 57-25, third place in the Western Conference behind San Antonio and the Lakers. Dallas took a six-game series from the Portland Trail Blazers in the first

---

[48] Ex-Mavs Coach Nelson Wins $6.3M in Arbitration Against Cuban. ESPN.com, August 1, 2008. Retrieved from http://sports.espn.go.com/nba/news/story?id=351 4135

round, then stunned the Lakers with a four-game sweep in the conference semifinals.

In the conference finals against Oklahoma City, Dallas won three straight by coming from behind in the fourth quarter each time to win the series 4-1. That set up an NBA Finals matchup with the Miami Heat. For Cuban, Nowitski and guard Jason Terry, the only two players remaining from the 2006 runner-up squad, it was a chance to avenge the bitter Finals defeat from five years prior. For the entire Dallas organization, it was an opportunity to shock a world that had already crowned the "Big Three" before the season began and to win its first championship.

After dropping the first game in Miami, the Mavericks were on the brink of falling behind two games to none when the Heat held a 15-point lead with 7 minutes left. But the Mavericks rallied and took the lead for good on a game-winning layup by Nowitzki with 4 seconds remaining.

Following that dramatic finish, Dallas won two of three games held in its home arena and clinched the series in Game 6, held in Miami.

In what was probably one of the greatest moments of his life, Cuban decided to step back. While it's customary for the commissioner to hand the trophy to the team's owner or top executive, Cuban instead allowed Donald Carter, who started the franchise, to accept the trophy on the team's behalf.

Mavs Fan For Life

Few people buy sports franchises as an investment. They are bought by fans who want to be part of the action. Cuban is different in that regard. While winning is the top priority, he has also turned the Mavericks into a viable business.

As the typical fan who identifies himself with his favorite teams, Cuban has always been a winner. There was perhaps no better place to grow up as a sports fan in the 1970s than Pittsburgh. The Steelers won four Super Bowls during Cuban's teenage years. The Pirates won the World Series in 1971 and 1979, with two other division titles during the decade. The NHL's Penguins fielded strong teams that consistently qualified for the playoffs.

The winning continued in college when his alma mater Indiana Hoosiers won the 1981 NCAA national men's basketball championship the year Cuban graduated. Things started out well his first years in Dallas, as both the Cowboys and Mavericks were perennial playoff contenders. But then the winning stopped for a time. The Cowboys suffered through several losing seasons, going 1-15 in 1989 before winning three Super Bowls in the 1990s.

That left the Mavericks, the team Cuban was most passionate about, having invested every year in season tickets. He signs his blogs MFFL, which stands for Mavs Fan For Life. The abbreviation is also on his vehicle license plates.

Having endured a decade of losing, Cuban wanted to field a winner immediately; there was no time for long-term rebuilding efforts.

Despite his role as a team owner, Cuban never shed his identity as a fan. Fans relate to him because in his soul, he's one of them. Obviously his billions of dollars in net worth puts him in a different social class. But Cuban doesn't behave like the "wealthy" fan. He doesn't sit courtside just to be seen. He doesn't treat the game like a social gathering with his country club friends or as the setting for closing his next business deal. Instead, he's truly engaged in the action happening on the court. He doesn't take up prime seats from a true fan, because he is a true fan. He appears to follow the Mavericks as a team more than he follows the team as a business. Just like any true fan, he shares, without any kind of filter, his opinion on what the Lakers should do with Kobe Bryant, or why he thinks the Miami Heat are the "evil empire."

Cuban berates the officials anytime a call goes against his team. If he wasn't one of the richest men in the world, one could easily picture the scruffy billionaire hanging out with his buddies at a Buffalo Wild Wings watching multiple sporting events at once, debating the greatest shooters in basketball and hitting on the waitress.

As the owner, Cuban has the authority to do what many fans wish they could: Storm into the locker room after a lackluster performance and lay in to the offending players, or inserting himself into the team huddle during games. And he can share his criticism of officiating with millions by talking to a reporter, tweeting to his 1.7 million followers or sharing his disgust on his blog.

At the same time, he represents a league that does not take kindly to his antics. While the average fan can yell whatever he wants to the officials, Cuban's criticism has cost him millions over the years. He once criticized the head of league officials by stating he how wouldn't trust the official to "manage a Dairy Queen." That drew the ire of both the league and Dairy Queen. But media savvy as he is, Cuban took the opportunity to work a day in a Dallas-area DQ, serving up cones and shakes to many appreciative Maverick fans.

With all of his success in his other ventures, Cuban's only failure, perhaps, is his inability to add to his sports empire. Cuban has attempted on several more occasions to mix business with sports. In 2006, he teamed with fellow Pittsburgh native and former NFL quarterback Dan Marino to bid $170 million for the Pittsburgh Penguins hockey franchise, but he was rejected.

Three years later, Cuban was prepared to spend a princely sum on one of the marquee franchises in all of professional sports: the Chicago Cubs.

"It's a team that represents so much to so many, with such a unique legacy, that when the opportunity arose, I decided to go for it," Cuban wrote in his blog on January 6, 2009.

Cuban really wanted to own the Cubs and thought his chances were good. He offered what he believed was a competitive price. One published report indicated that Cuban submitted the highest bid at $1.3 billion. Some claimed that Cuban never had a chance, regardless of his bid. The reason: Major League Baseball, like all the major sports leagues, have to approve any new team owners by a vote of the league's other owners.

Sources told ESPN that MLB owners feared Cuban would drive up player salaries by overspending for talent and exacerbate the gap between wealthy teams like the New York Yankees and Boston Red Sox and the league's also-rans. [49]

Cuban said that wasn't the case. He did desire to invest his resources to make the Cubs perennial contenders like he did the Mavericks, but at the same time did not want to spend as much on talent as the Red Sox and Yankees. He stated in his blog that he didn't want to pass on the expense of a bloated payroll to the team's loyalists. In fact, he believed he didn't have to spend that much, because he only had to compete with those clubs in a World Series. The rivals within the Cubs' division, the National League Central, were by and large not big spenders.

"My plans were to spend to win, not to spend for spending's sake," Cuban wrote in his blog. "[In my humble opinion], the money I could save being in the 2nd tier of payroll could be invested in scouting and development. I made this clear to any and all of the owners that I spoke to across the league. Of course that didn't stop some from trying to convince some owners otherwise."

---

[49] Report: 'Zero Chance' that MLB will Accept Cuban's Cubs Bid. ESPN.com, November 8, 2008. Retrieved from http://sports.espn.go.com/mlb/news/story?id=3687712

In the end, according to Cuban, his quest to buy the popular franchise ended because of the economic collapse of 2008. While Cuban may be a rabid fan, he's also an astute businessman. The adage of "buy low, sell high," applies to sports franchises.

He bought the Mavericks when they worth very little during a time when money was abundant. Trying to buy the Cubs in 2008 was the exact opposite; a franchise worth as much as it ever had been during a time when economic uncertainty carried the day. Before the financial crisis, Cuban was looking to finance the deal with short-term loans, then refinance at the end of each term, a common practice before the crisis. Once the crisis hit, there was no guarantee Cuban could refinance in a few years. His other option was to bring on more investors and pay cash for the Cubs. But he wrote in his blog that he was not about to spend that much in cash.

"Once the credit crisis hit, the value of cash went through the roof. It was not just a matter of how much the Cubs were worth, it was also a matter of how much more money I could earn with that cash. Cash was and is king," Cuban explained. "Distressed investment opportunities were rolling in the door that could make me multiples of what any sports team could. I could not see any scenario where the Cubs were worth anywhere near the numbers that had been discussed in the media." [50]

A year after that bid, Cuban and his investment group were outbid in an attempt to buy the Texas Ranger baseball team, which at the time was being auctioned by a bankruptcy court. Cuban was outbid by a group headed by former Rangers pitcher and Hall-of-Famer Nolan Ryan.

In 2011, the New York Mets, mired in the Bernie Madoff Ponzi scheme, were put up for sale. Cuban said he would consider jumping into the bidding only if the current owners called him; he wasn't going to chase it like he did his other baseball pursuits. In 2012, Cuban made another failed attempt to get into baseball by bidding for the Los Angeles Dodgers. Cuban was eliminated early in the process with a bid that was too low.

"The economics got so out of control because the Dodgers' TV deal's up for bid and so there's a lot of groups coming in going, 'This TV deal's worth so much money that we're gonna pay whatever it takes to get the Dodgers.' And so they're buying the TV

---

[50] The Cubs. Blog Maverick, January 6, 2009. Retrieved from http://blogmaverick.com/2009/01/06/the-cubs/

rights deal first and the team second," Cuban said at the time. [51]

Cuban also flirted with professional football, but not the big-time National Football League.

The United Football League was a four-team league that kicked off in 2009 in second-tier markets not served by the more established NFL. Cuban originally expressed interest in joining the UFL ownership group, but ultimately decided to limit his participation to broadcasting games on his HDNet network.

Cuban loaned the league money in 2011. This was at a time when the NFL and its players association were at a standstill in labor negotiations, which threatened to cancel some or all of the season. In the end, the NFL made peace with the players, and the UFL folded shortly later. Cuban filed a $5 million lawsuit to recoup the loan he made to the UFL.

Cuban loves sports. He also loves business and making money. Sometimes those two things are at odds. As much of a salesman as he is, and as much as he could charge for Mavericks tickets, the fan in him

---

[51] Cuban Explains Losing Out on Dodgers. CBSSports.com, January 30, 2012. Retrieved from http://www.cbssports.com/mcc/blogs/entry/22297882/34631046

wants everybody to have a chance to enjoy a live game every now and then. That explains why the Mavericks set aside 1,500 seats for 10 home games that sell for just $2, about the cost of a 20-ounce soda at a convenience store. Fans who attend games solo can buy their seat for as little as $5. [52]

Cuban eloquently wrote about the dichotomy between fan and businessman in one of his Maverick Blog posts:

> "When you own a professional sports team it doesn't take long to realize that owning a team is unlike owning any other business. On one hand the competitive side of ownership is a driving force. I want to win championships. I want to win every game. Not just for me, but for the entire organization and all of North Texas and for Mavs fans everywhere. Thirteen years into owning the Mavs and it still hurts every time we lose. I still have a hard time sleeping after any game we lose.
>
> But to some Mavs fans the Mavs are more than just a game. They are a release. They are a connection to other family members. They

---

[52] 20 Questions for Mark Cuban. Magbloom.com, February/March 2008. Retrieved from http://www.magbloom.com/wp-content/uploads/2012/02/20Q_bloom10.pdf

are an escape from the realities of a very difficult life. There are fans who love the Mavs because it makes their lives better. There are not many businesses that can begin to have that kind of impact on their customers/fans.

It is this connection that also drives me to make sure that every Mavs game is about far more than basketball. I want to make sure that every time any fan walks into the American Airlines Center they know that they will feel special. They will have a special experience. They will have an emotional connection... It is a special trust that is incumbent on me and all Mavs employees to live up to. It is expensive to deliver on this goal. But it is worth every penny. No matter what it costs. I'm proud of the fact that the Mavs spend, by all accounts, more than any other team in any sport around the world on in game entertainment and experience. While other teams worry about wi-fi and apps, we worry about creating an experience that is unique to Mavs games." [53]

---

[53] The Mavs are a Business Unlike Any Other. Blog Maverick, February 12, 2013. Retrieved from http://blogmaverick.com/2013/02/12/the-nba-is-a-business-unlike-any-other/

Chapter 6: The Investor

The 2008-2009 global financial crisis was unlike anything Mark Cuban had experienced in his professional and entrepreneurial career. Seemingly overnight, the economy tanked. Stocks lost tremendous value. Companies laid off millions. Home values plummeted. Interest rates bottomed.

To lift the nation out of the economic doldrums, government officials debated bailouts and stimulus packages. The key questions included: How much should the government dole out? What types of initiatives would have the best chance of jumpstarting the economy? How much debt could the country afford to tack on in order to lend a helping hand to corporate giants, small business owners, and unemployed workers?

As usual, Cuban had a different approach. He believed entrepreneurs were the key to leading the country out of its economic doldrums. And they didn't need billions in government funds to do it, either. In Cuban's mindset, they just needed a boost to get the momentum going.

So he turned his attention to helping others make their dreams come true. From his Maverick Blog, he announced the Mark Cuban Stimulus Plan. His stimulus plan was specifically designed to "inspire people to create businesses that could quickly become self-funding."

The plan worked like this: People posted their business plans on Cuban's blog. It didn't matter if others stole the idea. In his opinion, if it was good enough to steal, it was needed in as many places around the country as possible.

Cuban committed to investing in some of the ideas, but didn't put any minimum or maximum amounts in place. He did provide readers with a set of rules that would serve as the first hurdle in determining whether an idea received his financial attention. [54]

One of the first rules was that the business could not be advertising supported. As he explained in a follow-up interview, the reason for this strict rule was companies cannot depend on it: "I wanted to invest in companies with tangible products and services that could be sold for a profit. Sales is the lifeblood of any company. If you have a great product or service that is

---

[54] The Mark Cuban Stimulus Plan -- Open Source Funding. Blog Maverick, February 9, 2009. Retrieved from http://blogmaverick.com/2009/02/09/the-mark-cuban-stimulus-plan-open-source-funding/

differentiated and provides value, your entire focus can be on selling it." [55]

The company had to show break-even cash flow within 60 days and a profit within 90 days. Any month a business receiving funding didn't make its numbers, Cuban would turn off the spigot. Another rule was the business owner had to demonstrate that he or she would sell the product or service for more than it cost to produce. Also, the organization must be flat; no middle managers. The business plan had to indicate how much equity Cuban would receive or how he would earn a return on his investment.

"I make no promises that if your business is profitable, that I will invest more money. Once you get the initial funding you are on your own," Cuban wrote in the rules section. "I will make no promises that I will be available to offer help. If I want to, I will. If not, I won't."

Cuban has spent his post-Broadcast.com career serving as one of the country's leading angel investors, a term used to describe affluent individuals who provide capital to start-ups in exchange for an equity position or convertible debt.

[55] Bandyk, M. (2009). A New Kind of Stimulus Plan. U.S. News & World Report, 146(6), 75-76.

Helping the up-and-comer is part of his personal brand. He eschews large corporations and believes the best things are built one entrepreneur at a time. And while he's helping entrepreneurs get off the ground, he's collecting as well -- by potentially getting in on the ground floor of the next MicroSolutions or Broadcast.com, and without having to do much of the leg work. If an investment doesn't pan out, he's out a fraction of a percentage of his overall fortune.

As of March 2013, Forbes.com listed Cuban's net worth at $2.4 billion, ranking him 206 on the Forbes 400 list. [56]

Many of Cuban's investments have a technology slant. He has been involved by himself or with an investment group to provide financing recently to the following companies: [57]

- $1 million in a Florida company called LinguaSys, which provides linguistic engineering.

- $1.37 million in debt financing for uBeam, which has created a way to charge up portable electronic devices wirelessly.

---

[56] http://www.forbes.com/profile/mark-cuban/
[57] http://www.crunchbase.com/person/mark-cuban

- $800,000 for vidIQ, billed as the the first YouTube audience development and management suite that helps brands and agencies grow their views and subscribers.

- $1.5 million for Austin, Texas-based Insurance Zebra, a startup that aggregates car insurance quotes the way that Kayak aggregates flight and hotel deals.

- $1.6 million to San Francisco-based Clarity, which connects entrepreneurs with experts, over the phone, for advice on their business challenges.

- $1.85 million for Condition One, which develops next generation immersive video applications and provides an embeddable immersive video player for the iPad, which is licensed to media companies and brands.

- $1.75 million for a company called Upstart, a funding platform and mentoring network that matches students with backers who believe in their potential. Students can receive funding from Upstart to retire student loans, start a business or other uses, then share a percentage of their income with backers over 10 years.

- $1 million for Boston-based Apptopia, a marketplace for brokering mobile app acquisitions.

Mark Cuban's interests go beyond just high-tech. His website, markcubancompanies.com, details all of his various holdings, which include:

- Simple Sugars, an all-natural line of skincare products designed especially for sensitive skin, founded by an 18-year-old.

- The Game Face Company, which has a patented method for applying face paint, makeup and costume masks that makes the product easy to remove.

- KaZam Bikes, which a special bike to help younger children learn how to ride without the use of training wheels.

- Teddy Needs a Bath, a device that helps users clean stuffed animals.

- The Brondell Swash, an advanced toilet seat that provides users with warm water washes, adjustable heated seat, warm air dryer, automatic deodorizer and a wireless remote control.

One can't discuss Cuban's investment philosophy without detailing his most cunning investment decision. Had he not made this move, he likely would never have had the funds to invest in this stable of startups, and he certainly would not have enough to buy a basketball team or any other sports franchise.

When Yahoo! purchased Broadcast.com for $5 billion in April 1999, it paid for the transaction in Yahoo! stock, which at the time of the close of the sale was worth $145 a share. At its peak, the company was trading around $500 a share. However, part of the deal was that Cuban could not sell his shares for six months. Fearing that the company was overvalued and could quickly lose value -- costing him a fortune -- Cuban hedged his Yahoo! stock.

The hedge strategy Cuban used was a risk-reversal, which consists of selling a call and buying a put option. It's a complicated financial transaction, but it essentially protects against unfavorable, downward price movements. The downside is that it also limits how much profit you can earn when the stock price goes higher.

Call options gives you the right to buy a stock from the investor who sold you the option at a specific price on or before a specific date. For example, if you have a $35 call option on a stock and it rises about that mark before the option expires, you can pay $35 a share and essentially get discounted stock.

A put option works the opposite. You have right to sell a stock to an investor who sold you the option at a specific price on or before a specified date. So if you have a $25 put option and the stock falls below that mark, you can sell your shares for more than they're currently worth.

Though it cost Cuban $20 million up front to hedge his Yahoo! shares, the alternative would have been far worse. By the time he would have been able to sell the stock outright, according to the buyout agreement, the value of his holdings would have plummeted about 90 percent. The Mark Cuban story would have turned out much differently. [58]

The bottom line on this complicated transaction is that Cuban understood the risk of holding onto Yahoo! stock when it appeared likely to him that its value could dive. He didn't want to lose the fortune because of the whims of the market. He was more than willing to surrender a few million to hold onto his billions. He guessed right, and it wouldn't be the last time.

To Cuban, there's a huge difference between spending money and losing it. He has no problem handing out large tips, spending lavishly on clothes and cars and buying whatever he desires. That's the

[58] Leonard, D. (2007). MARK CUBAN MAY BE A BILLIONAIRE, BUT WHAT HE REALLY NEEDS IS RESPECT. Fortune, 156(8), 172-182.

beauty of being rich. What he can't stand is losing it and having nothing to show for the loss. That's why he's particularly selective about the types of investments he enters, and why he's so suspicious of the stock market.

For example, a business associate approached him in 2004 about investing in a hedge fund consisting of Private Investment in Public Equity (PIPE) funds. PIPEs invest directly into a public company through private deals in order to acquire stock at a discount. Companies, mostly small and medium-sized businesses, issue PIPE funds to raise needed capital. Cuban said no to this associate several times. In addition, he got out of any company that did PIPE deals.

Cuban turned out to be rightfully skittish. When the financial crisis struck in 2008, hedge funds couldn't get out of illiquid positions in microcap companies and they all crashed. [59]

Though he avoided investing in the offering, the pitch ended up nearly getting Cuban in trouble. In 2008, he was charged by the Securities and Exchange Commission with insider trading.

---

[59] How I Helped Mark Cuban Make a Billion Dollars and 5 Things I Learned from Him. The Altucher Confidential. Retrieved from http://www.jamesaltucher.com/2011/04/why-im-jealous-of-mark-cuban-and-5-things-i-learned-from-him/

According to the SEC's charges, Cuban sold 600,000 shares of a company called Mamma.com, a meta-search engine. The commission accused Cuban of selling the stock after learning of the company's PIPE offering through the aforementioned business associate. Rather than suffer dilution, the SEC claimed, Cuban sold the stock before the PIPE offering, saving himself $750,000. The case was eventually dismissed by a federal judge. [60]

Contrary to his sometimes buffoonish persona, Cuban is an extraordinary well-informed and insightful businessman. And like his philosophy on entrepreneurship, his concepts for fixing what he believes need repair are unique and often universally rejected by the powers-that-be.

For example, he has crusaded against certain stock market manipulations for some time:

> "Investors should be rewarded for actually owning companies and gaining returns on their investments. Financial engineers should have to pay a premium for the risk they introduce to the entire financial system. It was

---

[60] Schachter, K. (2008). UPDATE: Mark Cuban Charged With Insider Trading. Red Herring, 10.

not investors that brought on the last two crashes. It was the financial engineers.

The beautiful thing about this country is that we like to work hard, and we like to take chances. Unfortunately, over the last 15 years, the incentives have been to take chances as a financial engineer rather than as an entrepreneur. We give far more money to people who play games with financial instruments than we give to people who come up with ideas for the next big thing. That needs to change if we want to remain a leader in this world." [61]

During an appearance at his alma mater, Cuban told students gathered to hear him speak at Assembly Hall that the best thing they could invest in was themselves. When asked later to clarify that statement, Cuban responded:

"They wanted a stock tip. I told them that the dumbest thing they could do now is buy stock. There are no shortcuts to making money. The stock market is so big, and there

[61] Entrepreneurs, Investors and Financial Engineers -- Not All are "Business People." Blog Maverick, October 17, 2012. Retrieved from http://blogmaverick.com/2012/10/17/entrepreneurs-investors-and-financial-engineers-not-all-are-businesspeople/

are so many people involved in it, you have to get an intelligent advantage to make any money. It takes a lot of years of trial and error to get rich in the stock market. I told them to invest in sweat equity, to invest in themselves. Invest in equity that they understand and know better than anybody." [62]

Cuban is the type of person who doesn't stop at identifying a problem. He offers solutions. And in true Cuban fashion, they're quite different from the solutions proposed by the status quo.

To solve the problem of financial engineering and get people back to investing, Cuban proposes that there be no taxes on any gains from the sale of stock or bonds purchased, nor from dividends and interest, during an IPO and held for five years or more. He would not allow the stock to be borrowed against. Investors who sell during this five-year window would be taxed at their personal regular income tax rate. [63]

---

[62] 20 Questions for Mark Cuban. Magbloom.com, February/March 2008. Retrieved from http://www.magbloom.com/wp-content/uploads/2012/02/20Q_bloom10.pdf

[63] Entrepreneurs, Investors and Financial Engineers -- Not All are "Business People." Blog Maverick, October 17, 2012. Retrieved from http://blogmaverick.com/2012/10/17/entrepreneurs-investors-and-financial-engineers-not-all-are-businesspeople/

Cuban also once introduced the idea of hedge fund that placed sports bets instead of investing in stocks or bonds. The idea seemed to germinate less from an appreciation for sports gambling and more from his disdain of the public investment markets.

> "Unlike the stock market, you know the rules exactly. You know without question, the house is going to play by the rules. The gaming commission appears to actually enforce rules of play, unlike the SEC. And then there are sports bets. Like any other investment or bet, the question always come down to whether there is good information available, who knows how to use it better, and who is the competition and are they smart or not." [64]

Cuban never pursued the idea, largely due to an NBA prohibition on league representatives being involved in gambling. But another group did. In 2010, a London-based investment company named Centaur launched a hedge fund called Galileo. The fund's managers analyzed and traded the betting markets. [65]

---

[64] My New Hedge Fund. Blog Maverick, November 27, 2004. Retrieved from http://blogmaverick.com/2004/11/27/my-new-hedge-fund/

[65] Sports Betting Hedge Fund Becomes Reality. CNBC.com, April 7, 2010. Retrieved from http://www.cnbc.com/id/36218041

However, it only lasted a few years before going out of business for unspecified reasons. [66]

Despite his penchant for investing in the next big thing, Cuban also once expressed interest in getting into one of the oldest businesses: newspapers.

"Newspapers are a perfect example of how economics dominate common sense. Contrary to popular belief, newspapers aren't dying. Newspapers are making tons of money; they just aren't keeping their shareholders happy, they aren't meeting the expectations on Wall Street. The problem with newspapers is that they're trying to grow like they're Internet companies in 1999. Their shareholders are bitching at them about not showing growth in share prices. The minute you have to run your business for share prices, you've lost." [67]

Being a billionaire affords him the kind of freedom to chase what everybody else thinks is a lost cause. He doesn't have to take risks anymore. He doesn't need

---

[66] Sports Betting Hedge Fund Closes. ESPN.com, January 31, 2012. Retrieved from http://espn.go.com/blog/truehoop/post/_/id/36339/sports-betting-hedge-fund-closes

[67] What I've Learned: Mark Cuban. Esquire.com, November 17, 2008. Retrieved from http://www.esquire.com/features/what-ive-learned/ESQ1206BBCUBAN_182_1

the big score. He can spend on things he wants, and invest the rest conservatively, and the money will always be there. If he dumps a bunch of money into something like HDNet and never earns it all back, at least he spent it on something he enjoyed. And there's plenty more where that came from.

He's also free from the institutions he believes have the wrong motives. He will probably never take any of his companies public and put himself at the mercy of shareholders and directors watching over his shoulder.

> "If I'm making money, I'm happy. If we are profitable, great. If I make more than last year, great! It isn't like, 'Dang, I've got to grow 15 percent this year.' If I'm making money, if I'm paying my bills, I'm happy. Save a little bit, all the better. What's fucked up is, the people who run public companies don't think this way. They're just trying to get rich. The idea of running a public company isn't 'Wow, I can run a company.' It's 'Wow, I might be able to get rich!' Not just a-couple-million-dollars rich, but a-couple-million-dollars-a-year, fuck-you-money rich." [68]

---

[68] What I've Learned: Mark Cuban. Esquire.com, November 17, 2008. Retrieved from http://www.esquire.com/features/what-ive-learned/ESQ1206BBCUBAN_182_1

And by choosing not to chain himself to the public markets, Cuban doesn't have to behave himself for the sake of a stodgy board of directors and institutional investors. He can be himself at all times.

Chapter 7: The Celebrity

Mark Cuban originally retired at the age of 31, after selling MicroSolutions. He was a young multimillionaire who wanted to have fun.

So, of course, he landed in Hollywood.

Manhattan Beach, to be more specific. He spent $125,000 on a lifetime pass to fly anywhere on American Airlines, which he used to visit 11 countries. He bought a house on a whim. He partied, fornicated, and hung out at the beach. He also took acting classes and appeared in two movies in the mid 1990s. [69]

If you look them up on IMDB, you will find very little details on either, not even a plot synopsis. The first movie, released in 1994, was *Talking About Sex* starring Kim Wayans, sister of Keenen Ivory, Damon, Marlon and the rest of the Wayans comedy family. Cuban played a character named "Macho Mark."

---

[69] The Billionaire. Esquire.com, April 1, 2000. Retrieved from http://www.esquire.com/features/billionaire-cuban-sound-0400

In 1995, he appeared in a movie called *Lost at Sea*, a 90-minute R-rated action movie. The IMDB page for this flick lists five total cast members. The lead actor was Steve Sayre, whose biggest Hollywood credit is as the fight choreographer for the original Rocky. Cuban is listed in the film credits as "Villain." No other details about the movie are listed.

Since becoming a famous entrepreneur, sports team owner and billionaire, his occasional movie roles have still skewed to the obscure. He played a character named Seamus in the 2008 raunchy comedy, *One, Two, Many*, a $500,000 budget film about a guy trying to find a girlfriend who's OK with threesomes. He also had bit roles in the straight-to-video film *Like Mike 2: Streetball* (2002), and a cameo in *Tim and Eric's Billion Dollar Movie* (2012), which grossed a total of $201,000 at the box office.

The latter film was produced by 2929 Productions, Cuban's film company. The movie is a bizarre satire about two guys who get $1 billion to make a movie, only they squander most of the loot before they have a complete film made. In order to make the money back, they attempt to revitalize a shopping mall in decline.

One can hardly imagine other billionaires taking time out of their busy schedules to act in a raunchy sex comedy. Then again, he may be the only billionaire in the world who would provide commentary on his college debauchery, rather than try to hide it.

That's what happened when Deadspin.com discovered a photo gallery of his rugby playing exploits at Indiana on his Google+ profile. The site's editors asked him for permission to link the gallery. Not only did Cuban oblige, he wrote descriptions for those he could remember. [70]

One photo showed Cuban's friends being slid naked on a table toward a pyramid of cups, which Cuban called "rugger bowling." Another depicted Cuban laying on top of a woman with his rear end in her face, and another licking the face of a woman standing next to a friend. There was also one that captured what Cuban called the Indiana University 'elephant walk,' a ritual whereby naked men on their knees moved in a train formation. Cuban was not one of the participants in that photo.

These aren't the kinds of photos your average billionaire would be proud to show off. But then again, there is only one man that's almost universally considered to be "the coolest billionaire."

---

[70] "Hey, It Was The Seventies": Mark Cuban Narrates A Gallery Of His Debaucherous College Rugby Years. Deadspin.com, July 7, 2011. Retrieved from http://deadspin.com/5818693/hey-it-was-the-seventies-mark-cuban-narrates-a-gallery-of-his-debaucherous-college-rugby-years/

Mark Cuban loves the spotlight. He made five appearances, playing a fictionalized version of himself on the hit HBO show *Entourage* and played the role of Mark Smith in a two-part episode of the Chuck Norris drama *Walker, Texas Ranger* in 2000. He has appeared on *Real Time with Bill Maher*, *The Colbert Report*, *The Tonight Show*, and countless other talk and late night shows. He played himself in the updated TV series *Dallas*, a 2008 episode of the animated classic *The Simpsons*, and made a cameo on the HBO sports comedy *Arli$$*.

In December of 2007, Cuban guest hosted World Wrestling Entertainment's popular weekly television show, *Monday Night Raw*. He told wrestler Randy Orton that the only reason he won a wrestling match is because "these WWE refs are worse than NBA refs." Later in the evening, he got caught in a 'melee' between wrestlers and was thrown through a wooden table.

In 2010, the NBA All-Star Game was played in Dallas, and the hometown billionaire found a way to become the center of attention, yet again. He competed in the Celebrity All-Star Game, and one of his most memorable moments from the event was when Cuban had a shot rejected by actor Chris Tucker.

It's all part of the Cuban persona to want to be in front of the camera, even if just for a scene. That's why, even as a sports owner, he's better known than his players. And whereas most angel investors like to stay in the background, Cuban does much of his current investing in front of a national television audience as a panelist on ABC's *Shark Tank*.

In 2007, Cuban competed on *Dancing with the Stars*. Why would a billionaire who just had hip replacement surgery compete on a show reserved for has-been celebrities and retired athletes? "Because I can," Cuban wrote in his blog. Of course, he elaborates, offering even more insight into what make him tick:

> "It actually is more surprising to me that some people would even think twice if asked to participate on the show. I'm the first to admit that I'm the luckiest guy in the world. I can honestly say I wake up every morning with a smile knowing what a wonderful family, friends and life I have. It's the exact same way I felt when I was broke.
>
> Money makes so many things in life easier, but it can't buy you a positive outlook on life. Fortunately, how any of us approaches each of our days is completely up to us. It's not something you can buy or sell. It's not hard to

put a smile on your face every day, but for some reason some people find it impossible to do. Not me.

The opportunity to do something unique that makes me smile is something I try not to pass up. Dancing with the Stars is just that. It's not about how well I can dance. It's about the opportunity to compete at something I enjoy. It's about doing something that makes me smile every minute I'm doing it or even thinking about it. [71]

One interesting footnote to that appearance occurred five years later. He admitted in a radio interview that he was trying to work out a trade for Kobe Bryant during the rehearsals.[72]

Nowadays, Cuban is a regular on the ABC reality hit, *Shark Tank*. The show, which premiered in 2009, is a natural for Cuban, as it features business pitches from aspiring entrepreneurs to a panel of potential

---

[71] Dancing with the Stars and the Meaning of Life. Blog Maverick, September 7, 2007. Retrieved from http://blogmaverick.com/2007/09/07/dancing-with-the-stars-and-the-meaning-of-life/

[72] While on 'Dancing with the Stars' Mark Cuban Almost Traded for Kobe Bryant. CBSSports.com, August 22, 2012. Retrieved from http://www.cbssports.com/nba/blog/eye-on-basketball/19867305/while-on-dancing-with-the-stars-mark-cuban-almost-traded-for-kobe-bryant-

investors. Cuban became a panelist for a few episodes in season 2, then was inserted as a full-time cast member in season 3.

The show received a nomination for a Producers Guild Award in 2013. In 2012, *Shark Tank* received an Emmy nomination for Outstanding Reality Program and a nomination for a Critics' Choice Television Award for Best Reality Series.

In addition to Cuban, business owners looking for seed money also face real estate mogul Barbara Corcoran; "Queen of QVC" Lori Greiner; technology innovator Robert Herjavec; fashion and branding expert Daymond John; and venture capitalist Kevin O'Leary.

The panel has heard pitches on everything from beer-infused ice cream to pre-packaged meals for pets, a rent-a-grandma business, a fragrance that smells like money, and a spring-loaded laundry hamper, just to name a few.

> "Shark Tank is not scripted at all. When the entrepreneur walks into the shark tank the ONLY thing we know is their first name. NOTHING else.

> The only "scripted" part of the show is this... the producers tell us before every show... 'if an

entrepreneur looks like they are going to cry, shut up and let them.' They love tears. That's the only scripting.

We get the chance to do due diligence after the show. As a result, you uncover things that were not brought up in the show, so it's not unusual for a deal to fall through in the DD phase. I have had things like people who never paid their taxes, people who lied on the show, and people who didn't think that if they spent money on their personal credit cards it should be considered an expense. You name it.

There is so much pressure on the entrepreneur during the show that sometimes they say what they think we want to hear rather than the truth." [73]

In addition to being on a hit TV program, Cuban is also helping entrepreneurs through *Shark Tank*. Just for appearing on the show, contestants have to agree to give up a 5% equity stake or 2% of all future royalties to the producers. But several who have been on the program said it was worth it.

---

[73] Mark Cuban: What Entrepreneurs Need to Know Before Starting a Business. Entrepreneur.com, December 26, 2012. Retrieved from http://www.entrepreneur.com/blog/225357

Derek Pacque, a 24 year-old CEO who appeared on the show, told *Forbes* that his appearance had a major impact on his business. He founded CoatChex, a company that's developed a portable, automated system for checking coats and bags at events. He turned down an equity investment from Cuban when he appeared on the show. But after the episode aired, the company website received 1,000 hits per second. What's more, the company landed deals with American Express, NBC and Mercedes Benz, and it raised $200,000 in angel funding at better terms than what he was offered by the Sharks.

Likewise, 31-year-old Phil Dumas said the program helped him close a deal with a company he had long been in talks with. Dumas is the founder of UniKey, which has developed technology to connect smartphones with door locks. [74]

"I try to quickly decide if I'm investing in the business or the person," said Cuban. "From there I can determine whether I want to own the business, or

---

[74] Is 'Shark Tank' Really Worth 5% of Your Company? Business Owners Say 'Absolutely.' Forbes.com, June 13, 2013. Retrieved from http://www.forbes.com/sites/jjcolao/2013/06/13/is-shark-tank-really-worth-5-of-your-company-business-owners-say-absolutely/

whether it's an inexpensive way to hire someone smart to run the business." [75]

Not all of Cuban's reality TV efforts have been hits. In 2004, he launched *The Benefactor*. The premise was 16 contestants competed to win $1 million from Cuban based on his assessment of their skills during weekly tasks. The show never found an audience, despite being the lead-in to Monday Night Football, and was cancelled after just one month on the air.

A quote attributed to Cuban illuminates, perhaps, the root of his need for attention. Back in 1997, a company called Reset was getting in the business of live streaming of TV shows. AudioNet contacted the company because it wanted Reset to use its technology to do the live streaming. A salesperson pleading his case to the executives at Reset said: "Mark Cuban wants to go public and we NEED press releases. Press releases drive IPOs. This would be a great press release." [76]

---

[75] Mark Cuban, Billionaire (Scared, Broke and Jobless). Subvert Magazine, September 10, 2012. Retrieved from http://www.subvertmagazine.com/blog/mark-cuban/

[76] How I Helped Mark Cuban Make a Billion Dollars and 5 Things I Learned from Him. The Altucher Confidential. Retrieved from http://www.jamesaltucher.com/2011/04/why-im-jealous-of-mark-cuban-and-5-things-i-learned-from-him/

Companies need publicity. Brands need publicity. Any kind of publicity. Any kind of attention. All of Cuban's major holdings, from the Mavericks to 2929 Productions to AXS TV owe much of their success to the Mark Cuban brand and the ideas that brand generates.

The Mark Cuban brand needs to stay in the public eye. It needs to forge and reinforce a certain reputation. It needs to reach a certain audience and create buzz. Because without a strong and viable Mark Cuban brand, the companies he owns and pumps money into likely wouldn't continue to thrive. At least not in the way they have.

Magic? The golden touch? Whatever "it" is, Mark Cuban has it!

Chapter 8: The King

The title of this final chapter doesn't mean to imply that Mark Cuban is royalty. In fact, his anti-establishment ways would shun any comparison to nobility. And it isn't because he's one of the richest men in the world. Instead, the title 'king' summarizes, in one word, the life of Mark Cuban, who always has and always will be the king of his world, his destiny and his life.

If you had to summarize the life of Mark Cuban, one way would be to divide it in thirds.

The first third encompasses the early struggles. He grew up in a middle class family in Pittsburgh. His father, Norton, worked as an automobile upholsterer. Mark was your run-of-the-mill Jewish kid, not a genius but not a slacker either; not popular but not a bullied nerd. He never wanted for basic needs, never experienced poverty, but lived a life when a meal at restaurant was a special occasion. It wasn't a bad life, but it was far less than he desired for his adulthood. He used to drive through ritzy neighborhoods admiring the stately houses, telling himself that the people living in those castles worked hard to get there. If they could do it, he told himself over and over, so could he.

He was lured to Dallas from a stable job in Indiana. He had nothing with him when he drove a 1977 Fiat X19 with a hole in the floorboard and leaking oil to the heart of the Lone Star State. He arrived in the city of J.R. Ewing and the Dallas Cowboys with dreams as big as Texas.

He moved into a tiny three-bedroom apartment with five friends struggling to make a living. He had no bedroom, not even a bed to sleep on or a closet or dresser to store what few clothes he brought. He drank from $12 bottles of champagne while he tended bar, waiting for his big break.

"I never thought of packing it up and moving home. Not one single time," said Cuban. "I just knew I had to figure it out. The only person I would depend on was me. I wasn't always optimistic. There were times when I got scared. I was broke. I had no job. But I kept on pushing. I wasn't going to quit. After all I had nothing to lose. All I had was what I had and it wasn't much." [77]

---

[77] Mark Cuban, Billionaire (Scared, Broke and Jobless). Subvert Magazine, September 10, 2012. Retrieved from http://www.subvertmagazine.com/blog/mark-cuban/

The middle third is when he made his first million and then first billion by doing all the things he espouses to others. He went after his dreams. He worked hard. He pursued his passions. And he cashed in not once, but twice -- building valuable properties in MicroSolutions and Broadcast.com.

When a blogger tried to make the case that Cuban is not a visionary, but just lucky, he responded:

> "Yeah Im lucky. And proud to be. I was lucky with MicroSolutions when we started selling LANs in 1983 before anyone else and sold to Compuserve. I was lucky selling corporate business applications I wrote and developed. I was lucky with Precept, a hedge fund built on my tech background that I sold (didn't know about that one did you.). I was lucky with Broadcast.com, I was lucky to start HDNet years before anyone else thought HD had a chance, lucky with about 10 other companies, too. [78]

The last third may best be described as the evolution of the Mark Cuban brand. In the world of marketing, all brands evolve over time. Those that can't change

---

[78] Mark Cuban 1, Loren Feldman 0. Techcrunch.com, August 28, 2008. Retrieved from http://techcrunch.com/2008/08/28/mark-cuban-v-loren-feldman-cuban-wins/

with the rapid pace of innovation and advancement eventually cease to exist. Cuban has adjusted his brand to account for his older age, his relatively new responsibilities as husband and father of three, and the changing world around him.

> "I mean, I don't think I'm all that different than before. Money doesn't show up in how I dress. It doesn't show up in what I do or where I go or how I act. It just makes life simpler. I was happy when I was broke and I'm happy now.
>
> What defines me is nothing I ever think about. It's not like, what's my legacy going to be, or how do people think about me, or don't they know this about me or that about me. I don't pay attention to that at all. If anything defines me it's how my kids turn out. That's the only important job I have." [79]

Cuban is much different on the outside in this third act of his life than he was in the first two. He's made a fortune, become famous, and won an NBA championship. The now 54-year-old has a net worth of $2.4 billion as of March 2013, which ranks him

---

[79] 20 Questions for Mark Cuban. Magbloom.com, February/March 2008. Retrieved from http://www.magbloom.com/wp-content/uploads/2012/02/20Q_bloom10.pdf

613th on Forbes list of the world's billionaires, 213th in the United States. Anything more he would accomplish from this day forward would be gravy on top of an already remarkable life.

Does Mark Cuban still have the drive and determination that he did before? In some ways yes, in others, no.

Early on in this third stage, Cuban continued to do everything he could on a grand scale. He hired John Mellencamp to entertain guests at a barbeque shortly after he cashed out on the Broadcast.com deal. When he married longtime girlfriend Tiffany in 2002, the bachelor party guests were flown from three different cities in Cuban's private plane, supplied with alcohol and female dancers, to Las Vegas. The couple's wedding reception took place in American Airlines Arena, with rock legend Sammy Hagar providing the entertainment.

> "The best thing about the money, I guess, is that I don't have to prove myself anymore. There are some guys you talk to, they want to move up the list. They're like, I'm shooting for the top twenty, the top ten, whatever. I don't need to move up the fuckin' list. I'm the first to realize that my success is yesterday's news. But I'm not necessarily concerned about thinking, 'Can I do it again?' What's more

important to me is: Can I find something new that consumes me, that entertains me to the same extent, that challenges me in the same way? It's the never-ending question, I guess."
80

Wealth may have changed Cuban on the outside, but it did little to alter his heart and motivations. He still eats roast beef sandwiches, likes to go to movies, and worries about his weight like any other middle aged man. He remains loyal to the friends he partied with at Indiana University and crashed with in his first Dallas apartment.

Mark Cuban lives like a king because he can essentially do what he wants, the laws of his state and country notwithstanding. He has the money to do anything, go anywhere or buy whatever his heart desires. He has maintained independence from the institutions that want their billionaire CEOs to act in a dignified manner. And since he has no interest in ever running for public office, there's no harm in sharing tasteless college photographs with the world.

He competed on *Dancing with the Stars* not because he had to, but because he could. He shared the

---

80 The Billionaire. Esquire.com, April 1, 2000. Retrieved from http://www.esquire.com/features/billionaire-cuban-sound-0400

proceeds of the sale of Broadcast.com with its employees not because he had to, but because he could. He spent a day working at a Dairy Queen not because he had to, but because he could. Few people in his position could get away with hanging out in a bar with college students a few days before the Super Bowl, but Mark Cuban can.

"I mean, some people can run to freedom," Cuban says. "I can sell to freedom. And that's what I learned when I was a kid. Time and freedom. Those are the ultimate assets, absolutely. My self-fulfillment doesn't come from the money. It comes from just knowing that intellectually there are no bounds--that's the number-one thing. Nobody telling me what to do. Just me doing things because I can." [81]

Another thing he can do with his wealth and fame is help others. Whether it's the natural progression of a maturing man, the result of having a family of his own, some atonement of past sins or simply because he has the means, Mark Cuban is spending a lot of money simply helping others. And not all of it is in the traditional charitable sense. The irony is that he virtually built his fortune on his own, save for the investments of his various business partners.

---

[81] The Billionaire. Esquire.com, April 1, 2000. Retrieved from http://www.esquire.com/features/billionaire-cuban-sound-0400

For example, in February 2013, Cuban announced that he wanted a new uniform for the Mavericks from the 2015-16 season. But he wasn't hiring a professional design or branding firm to draw the new threads. He solicited all comers through his blog to submit design ideas. If he found one he liked, he would use it. As with many of his offers to help up-and-comers, Cuban made no promises that any of the submitted ideas would be used. [82]

That initiative fits with one part of the Mark Cuban brand that will always stay constant: his belief that the best ideas come from individuals, not companies.

He has also used his popular blog to encourage men to their colons examined, and he did it in typical Mark Cuban fashion.

> "I'm getting to that age where it pays to be proactive and start getting tested for the myriad of things that can go wrong with my body. One of the things I wanted to get over with is a check for colon cancer. Although I'm officially younger than the 'suggested age' for a colonoscopy, I wanted to get it out of the

---

[82] Help the Mavs Design Our Next Uniform! Blog Maverick, May 13, 2013. Retrieved from http://blogmaverick.com/2013/05/13/help-the-mavs-design-our-next-uniform/

way. I had read and heard too many stories about people who found polyps and how if they had only caught them a little sooner it would be no big deal to remove them. So I set my appointment and went for it."

"I was definitely nervous. Despite doctors and nurses telling me it would be a breeze, I was naturally skeptical. A breeze was an overstatement. I can honestly say that if it made medical sense to get one done every year, I would have no problem with it. It was easy and breezy.

Once I got into the Gastro Room where they did these, they told me that they were going to knock me out, and I would get a nap and wake up like nothing happened. They were right. One minute I'm talking rugby, the next I'm waking up, picking up the conversation where I left off and being told to 'dispell the air in my system.'

No where else can you rip off some huge farts and have 3 nurses and a doctor, while maintaining a very professional demeanor, tell you that you aren't done yet and demand that you let loose a few more. Then it was up to get dressed and out the door so my wife could give me a ride home."

"Bottom line is that your life just might depend on getting tested for colon cancer. There is absolutely nothing to be afraid of. It's truly easy and breezy. Do it." [83]

In addition to his investment in startups and his investments in investigative journalism, Cuban has also become a philanthropist. Shortly after the Iraq War started, Cuban created the Fallen Patriot Fund to help families of killed or wounded soldiers. The fund has provided $2.6 million to families of soldiers.

"I don't think I've ever taken it for granted that anything I've accomplished is all because my grandparents, my parents, our friends have fought. And kids today are out there fighting to make sure all of us here have that opportunity. Before every game during the national anthem, I say to myself 'thank you' to everybody who fought before and everyone fighting now to keep this country so great. And when we invaded Iraq I was finally in a position to put my money where my mouth was. We started the Fallen Patriot Fund so I could at least try to help.

---

[83] My Colonoscopy. Blog Maverick, June 14, 2007. Retrieved from http://blogmaverick.com/2011/09/10/my-colonoscopy-2/

Actually, the Fallen Patriot Fund is the only one of my foundations that I've publicly put my name on. For me to give money to anybody else, one of the requirements is that you have to be anonymous, because I don't ever want to think I'm giving money to get PR. I want to always make sure I'm doing it because that's the reason I want to do it. I'll promote the Fallen Patriot Fund, but even then, you don't see me going out there and talking about it a lot. It stands on its own. We've been able to raise enough and I've contributed enough that we've been able to cover expenses. And if we were ever to run short, then I'd put up my own money. That's the way it works." [84]

A key difference between the Cuban of old and the older Cuban is how thinly he's spread compared to his early years.

He focused all of his efforts on MicroSolutions and then on Broadcast.com. Now he has a sports team, a TV network, motion picture business, a chain of movie theaters, a production company, TV

---

[84] 20 Questions for Mark Cuban. Magbloom.com, February/March 2008. Retrieved from http://www.magbloom.com/wp-content/uploads/2012/02/20Q_bloom10.pdf

appearances, and a slew of other companies in his investment portfolio.

Without Cuban's 100 percent focus, do any of them have a chance to become the next big thing?

Certainly, fortunes don't grow as fast as they used to. Much of the rest of the world has caught up to Cuban's methods. There are more ideas, but less money.

While he does acknowledge that he lacks the time to add much else to his portfolio, he has expressed some interest in trying to turn around the newspaper industry, which follows the rule of doing something that nobody else wants to be part of. Perhaps Amazon founder Jeff Bezos' recent decision to acquire *The Washington Post* will tempt Cuban to get into the game.

Another sign the world of Mark Cuban is different: He used one of his blog posts to explain a joke he made on a podcast with ESPN's popular sports columnist, Bill Simmons, aka "The Sports Guy." Simmons and Cuban were debating the merits of the "The Kiss Cam," a staple at most sporting events in which a camera will fixate on a couple, who are then supposed to kiss while the rest of the stadium or arena watches. Simmons said he loved "Kiss Cam," to which Cuban replied, "That's because you and your boyfriend are always on it."

"I made a mistake in making the comment. I wasn't trying to be hurtful. It wasn't a comment on anyone's sexuality. It was just me trying to be funny. It wasn't. I quickly realized it and tried to fix it. I hoped at the time I didn't offend anyone.

This blog post is not about trying to defend what I said. I'm not trying to defend my sense of humor. I'm not trying to convince you I'm not a homophobe. I'm not trying to justify anything at all.

I guess what I am doing is admitting that at some level I am prejudiced and that I recognize that I am. There are a lot of things in my life that I need to improve at. This is one of them. Sometimes I make stupid throw away comments that I quickly realize are wrong. It doesn't happen often, but it happens. It was a mistake and I realized it. I learned from it.

I'm the last to be politically correct and the last thing I am trying to be here is politically correct. I honestly don't give a shit what you think about me. But I think being the person

I want to be includes not blurting out throw away jokes about sexuality, race, ethnicity, size, disability or other things people have no say in about themselves. I'm the guy who still feels bad about punching Michael Cooper in the stomach in 6th grade purely because he was overweight, even though I made the point to apologize to him when I ran into him at a reunion years later.

Even if I don't care about you, it doesn't mean I'm ok with making you uncomfortable or upset with a comment that references anything that is out of your control. That is not the person I want to be.

I'm happy to pick on you if you root for the wrong team. I'm happy to pick on you if you like doing The Wave. I'm happy to pick on you for a lot of reasons. Your sexuality should never be one of those reasons.

I like who I am. I love my life. But that doesn't mean I won't always try to be a better version of me. And yes, I feel better having written this blog post." [85]

---

[85] Am I a Homophobe? Blog Maverick, March 9, 2012. Retrieved from http://blogmaverick.com/2012/03/09/am-i-a-homophobe/

But unlike other celebrities' brands that have crumbled because of saying the wrong thing with a camera or recorder going, Mark Cuban's brand has survived and continued to thrive. That may be because his brand is grounded in the ideals of the common American: Cheer for the underdog, give the person willing to work hard a fair shot, and run a business for the benefit of you and your customers, not shareholders and governments.

He's not trying to impress stuffed shirt executives or conservative investors. He's reaching out to people like him: people with dreams, people with energy, people with creativity, people with determination and people with no fear.

A reader of his blogs and the hundreds of articles written about him would be hard pressed to find any mention of a professional mentor. There seems not to exist a person that a young Mark Cuban looked up to, nobody who can take even partial credit for molding him, teaching him the ways of business or helping him learn from his own mistakes. There is plenty of mention of the bosses who pushed him into entrepreneurship because of what Cuban believed was their incompetence as managers.

In all of Cuban's interviews, blog posts and book excerpts, one quote seems to encapsulate everything in this book and everything about the way Mark Cuban has lived his life to this point. It's the concluding sentence to a blog post he wrote in 2007 titled "Dancing with the Stars and the Meaning of Life."

"When I'm 90 years old and talking to my grandkids and hopefully great-grand kids, I won't be the grandparent who tells them about the things I wished I had done and how they should experience life, I will be the grandparent with tons of great stories that hopefully inspires them to live their lives to the fullest." [86]

---

[86] Dancing with the Stars and the Meaning of Life. Blog Maverick, September 7, 2007. Retrieved from http://blogmaverick.com/2007/09/07/dancing-with-the-stars-and-the-meaning-of-life/

30541834R00081

Made in the USA
Lexington, KY
08 March 2014

DEALERS

By **Peter Madsen**

Cover art by **Christy Karacas**

pH **powerHouse Books** Brooklyn, NY

To my parents. And Fuzz.

*The criminal class is a more exact cross-section
of humanity than any trade could be.*

—Luc Sante
in interview with *The Believer*

TABLE OF CONTENTS

The story behind this collection of anonymous interviews with New York City drug dealers, which I conducted during the last half of 2012 and early 2013, begins four years earlier, when I was laid off from a media company I had moved to New York to work for. Then in my mid 20s, outgrowing youth culture yet lacking any genuine perspective of my own (and, therefore, anything worth writing about), I bought a $100 bike on Bedford Avenue (*ahem*) and did a lot of riding around. I so much loved exploring New York on two wheels I eventually took up work as a messenger. Few other occupations (save perhaps cab driving, high-rise window-washing, or—yikes—being a cop) can so thoroughly familiarize someone to the humanity that resides in New York.

After months of riding without writing I itched to publish again but I was still unsure of what I had to offer. Instead of straining to be just another blogger, I decided to leave the observations to others: mostly panhandlers. When someone asked if I could spare a buck, I'd instead offer $10 for a snapshot and a quick interview about a sometimes observational yet invariably simple, humanist topic: "Why do you have tattoos on your face?" "What's the most difficult thing you've explained to a child?" "Can wife-beaters be good people?" Thus began Word on the Street

New York dot com, where I've archived over 250 such interviews with people whose words always defy expectations.

It was this project that caught the attention of powerHouse Books, and while they passed on "WotSNY" (hey, they have first option hereafter) they did take interest in some people I would incidentally interview now and again: dealers. While *Dealers* retains the same conversational tone of WotSNY, the subjects and I aren't rushed by my need to get to my next pick up; instead we have the time to let the interactions take us where they might. As an interviewer I'm enduringly interested in the subject as the ultimate authority on his experience, and I think one's attention to detail may be that much more acute when his daily existence depends on an illegal, stigmatized, and consequently very secretive trade. For that, I was gratified to find that my subjects' need to speak to and be understood by people who live outside (but not above) this underworld was pronounced. After many late-hour meet ups, a few obligatory transactions (OK, not *that* obligatory), and several days-worth of audio later (the iPhone 4S is a great voice recorder), I am very pleased to present the following interviews with people whom, for worse or perhaps much better, are *Dealers*.

Peter Madsen

MIGUEL

34, Flatiron

Are you a drug dealer?

Ah, no. I'm a concierge at a large luxury building.

Oh. So do you know any drug dealers?

Drug dealers who go through here? Yeah. You can tell a drug dealer when he comes in. Personally, a lot of my friends are dealers. You can tell with escorts, as well.

And you let them in?

Of course! It's a matter of someone having invited a guest and my letting him upstairs. I mean, of course I will call the tenant and announce the person. But that's it. I'm not here to judge people. Here's how you can tell a drug dealer: If you have a tenant who is kind of a preppy guy and his friend's décor is very "urban," you can just tell they're not really friends-friends. He comes and goes within five minutes and you know what obviously happened. It's not like a doorman is blind to it.

You're saying you can tell they sell drugs by judging their appearance?

Pretty much.

Do dealers who specialize in certain drugs dress in certain ways?

Well, yeah. A lot of weed dealers appear as bike messengers, for example. Or you'll have a guy—I don't know how to best put this in PC terms—who comes from an "urban background."

You mean a black or Spanish ghetto?

A black or Spanish ghetto. And they'll wear hip-hop gear. Usually those are the guys who are selling *that.*

Cocaine.

Yeah, and they dress like they're from the Bronx or something.

So these weed messengers always wear bags?

They always have bags and they always have that look that's perhaps less a bike-messenger look as an I-live-in-Williamsburg look. Of course, it's a whole different ballgame when it comes to synthetics. That doesn't really happen so much around here.

Synthetics?

You know, like OxyContin. That's more private. But when it comes to dealers coming in on the regular, yeah, you notice them.

Do the guys who sell coke wear bags?

No, no. Rarely will they carry anything at all. I mean, there's not too much for them to carry anyway. They just come in nonchalant.

How do they regard you?

For the most part they're OK. They don't want to bring trouble to themselves. Actually, it's good you brought that up. I would say with the bike messengers, those guys are a lot more respectful. They know how to play the game. With the coke guys, I think because their world is more intense, sometimes they'll get frustrated when I stop them and call the resident first—but that practice is standard. I mean, that's what our job is. But for the most part, they're OK.

Is their world more intense because of the greater consequences for getting caught with coke?

It's a matter of what that world does to you. Because it's coke, you get more of a high-octane energy off them. Not just from the dealer, but from the residents who are into that stuff as well. The dealers are that much more *tense*.

Are certain hours busier than others?

You rarely see these guys during the day, but once the sun goes down, that's it. That's when you start seeing them. During the holidays I get a lot more, too. It's the holiday anxieties that bring it on. Between work—everyone's trying to get everything done before the end of the year—you've got Christmas gifts… It's all this crap that comes along with it. And what also comes with all of that is a lot more partying. People party *a lot harder* during the holidays.

Do you think non-drug-ordering residents recognize the dealers as such?

No, no. They wouldn't even notice at all.

That someone who comes from a different background is coming into their luxury building?

No, because there's always a lot of guest traffic of different backgrounds. Especially here in New York City where everything is so international and cluttered with every type of culture and class. If anything they'll probably be upset—OK, maybe not *upset*—that they're sharing an elevator with someone who is living in a low-income apartment. That's probably how they would view them.

Why doesn't the NYPD just wait outside luxury buildings and stop the people who don't fit in?

It would be complicated for a cop. First of all, it would be illegal. Let's suppose it's your apartment, and you're inviting your "guest" over. The cop didn't see any transaction or exchange. He would have nothing to go on.

What if a cop detains a drug dealer as he leaves the building and he wants to question you about the guy?

I would tell him that the man just went upstairs as an invited guest. That's all. Again, I am not one to judge who goes upstairs and what goes on in anyone's apartment. Whatever you do in your apartment is your business. You could bring up sheep, for Christ's sake.

I'm sure there a law against that. How often do residents ask you if you "know a guy"? Do you put them in touch?

Yeah, of course. All the time. Some people are too embarrassed or they already know someone. But a couple times a week there are some people who ask me and I will connect them with my friends. Or my friends' friends.

What time of day do people ask? How do they appear?

After they feel comfortable with me they open up. I don't see anything wrong with [referring them to drug dealers]; granted, it's illegal, but at the same time, people are going to find it sooner or later, someway, somehow. So why not help one friend make money and help another be happy? I'm just the middleman. That's all.

You're the connect.

That's right.

So you know a guy for pot?

Yeah.

And you know a guy for coke?

Yeah, almost everything.

A guy for MDMA?

Molly? Yeah.

LSD?

Yeah.

PCP?

Not too many people do that, but, I mean, I could make a couple phone calls and I'll find it in a day.

Crack?

Yeah, that too.

Heroin?

You know what? I have never been asked for that. Also LSD. Nobody really does any of that stuff here.

DMT?

I've never been asked for that. That's some weird stuff.

Methamphetamine?

Oh, hell no! This ain't Wisconsin! Fuck no.

Meth has popularity among certain gay men.

Yeah, that's true.

How about bath salts?

Hell no. That's super new.

Would you ever worry about someone going through one of your referrals, having an overdose or a really bad reaction to the drug, and that coming back to you? Whether they cause damage to their apartment or they become violent with other residents?

It's happened before to be honest with you. This one guy OD'd. To a certain extent, I do feel guilty. I never want someone to go that far.

Did he die from the OD?

No, he died from alcohol poisoning. I feel remorseful and I felt guilty when that occurred. He was an alcoholic. But he wanted some snow, so I called a friend.

Did this resident buy a large quantity?

Yes, an 8-ball.

That's 3.5 grams.

Right. I'm so oblivious to this stuff. So the thing with this guy is he was borderline autistic in the sense that he was a brilliant guy. He worked for Goldman Sachs, Credit Suisse—all the big guys down there. He had an addictive personality; he would overdo it. So this one time he was on this binge and he asked me for some nose candy and I was reluctant. I said, "No, dude, I'm not going to get that for you, especially in your condition." But he offered me $2,000 on top of whatever it was for the 8-ball.

Just to be the middleman?

$2,000. I said OK.

How long after he got the 8-ball did he die?

Three weeks later. It really affected me a lot. That's the reason I changed buildings, in fact. He was a nice guy. But dude, if someone offers you $2,000 just to make a phone call? I was just like, "All right. Fuck it." [Shrugs, looks down.]

Were you working when he died?

Yeah. One of us went upstairs to check up on him and found him already dead. The maintenance guys were just mortified. So I went up there, checked his pulse. His neck was bent against the kitchen wall. There was vomit on his shirt, and he was purple. In his apartment he had four empty liters of vodka that he had just downed. So he was just going in a spiral, all the way down.

Do you think he committed suicide?

It could have been. I think it was more that he just didn't care. We tried to help him out as much as we could. As a matter of fact, his hedge fund had actually sent him out to one of the best rehab centers in Connecticut where each night costs some exuberant amount. He came out fresh and clean. There were times I would go upstairs and we'd chat. He had plans for the future. But, as they say with alcoholics, it's a disease they just can't get away from. I don't know what triggered it. I was on vacation when he started going downhill. The demon just got to him.

Did you tell your drug dealer friend what happened?

Yeah. I wouldn't say he didn't care, but he was just like, "Well." That was his only word.

When the cops came were you worried about them finding drugs in his apartment?

I don't think there were any. I mean, I didn't see any. I didn't get the toxicology report, but I don't think the 8-ball contributed to his death. But I wasn't worried at all that I would be implemented. I did contribute to him going out there, but he would have found coke through someone else. But I didn't think he would die. He had spiraled out before, but he would always freshen up. Some people binge.

Would he ever misbehave?

Sometimes he would blast music in his apartment.

What kind of music did he like?

He was a big Springsteen fan. [Chuckles.] He was your classic rock guy.

Do a lot of your residents do drugs?

No. I would say a little less than 30%.

That's a sizable minority!

Well, "drugs" is such a broad term these days. It could be doctor-prescribed drugs.

Do you do drugs with any of your residents?

Yeah, I'll smoke up. That's it. Coke has been offered but I don't participate too much in that. As chummy as I get with residents, I am aware I am still an employee, and something like that could come back to bite me in the ass.

You wouldn't ever do a key bump?

No. Not unless there was a hot chick. Then maybe. But coke is not my thing.

Has a resident ever turned a dealer away?

No. I've seen call girls refused, but not dealers. Usually the resident wants them there as soon as possible—especially the coke guys.

How do you know so many drug dealers?

I grew up in Washington Heights. I grew up with it. In the 80s and 90s it was a big coke/crack location because you have the George Washington Bridge right there, and people would come from New Jersey for the drugs. I remember playing baseball or basketball in the street and guys with Jersey plates would drive up and say, "Hey, do you know where I could get some crack?" Two of my cousins are actually serving time upstate after the Rockefeller Drug Laws and some other stringent laws came into play.

Why aren't you a drug dealer?

[Laughs.] I want to live. Fuck that, dude. Look how skinny I am. In prison I would be a bitch.

Avoid prison and just run weed.

[Pause] I could but if I wanted to do that I would have done that years ago, and I just didn't want to get into that business. There's no 401(k) in that. Sure, now there is a gold rush with weed but I'm too much of a pussy to get involved in that. And believe me, I was recruited, hired even—

So you were once a drug dealer.

Briefly, but I was the worst coke dealer because I had to find customers and I don't like imposing on anyone. A friend of mine wanted me to sell because I was working in the dance music industry and I knew people who were into coke. But I'm not comfortable with hanging out with my friends and saying, "Hey, do you want to buy some drugs?" because it just changes our category from friends to dealer-customer. I just didn't want the problems with that shit.

If you rarely make money by being a middleman, why do you put people in touch?

Well, it's just one of the many services I provide as a concierge. Anyway, the residents hit me back come Christmastime.

CHICO 117

30s, Harlem

How long have you been selling drugs?

[Laughs very hard.] Oh god, off and on since I was 17.

Do your parents know you sell drugs?

Yes. [Laughs.]

Are they upset?

No.

Why not?

My father was a hustler, so whatever.

What did he hustle?

Weed, same shit as me.

Did you grow up aware of this?

Yeah, fully aware. My dad used to sell pounds. There would
be like a pound in the living room at all times.

Just hanging out on the coffee table?

Yeah, he used to smoke mad weed and there would be mad
scales around.

**How old were you when you figured out all this was
remarkable?**

When I was in kindergarten I knew what was going on and
knew I wasn't supposed to talk about it. When I went to other
people's houses, it wasn't like that. [Laughs.] My dad had
money and shit, we had money growing up. Had a car, a
duplex apartment.

What kind of car?

My pops had a Honda, it was no big deal. We lived in Spanish
Harlem, Uptown in Manhattan, and not everybody had a car—
maybe ten in the building.

**How did you know not to talk about this stuff with your
friends?**

My parents never hid shit from me. They would tell me that
I'm not supposed to tell people because it's illegal and we'd
get in trouble for it—but that's how we eat. [Laughs.]

**So if someone asked what your dad did, what would you
say?**

A fisherman. [Laughs.]

A fisherman?

He used to work on shrimp boats and shit, but I guess he found a connect and stopped.

He was living in Harlem and would go shrimping?

He would go away for months and come back. We'd get giant boxes of shrimp in dry ice sent to the house.

Is your dad a big, brawny guy?

[Laughs.] No, he is a fucking pretty boy! I don't even understand how he did shit like that. It's weird, I try to be like him all the time.

You do?

Yeah, good looking and manly. [Laughs.] Like having nice clothes, but you can change a flat and build a house basically.

So did your dad ever get in trouble?

He got locked up in Alabama for transporting weed. He had a bunch of pounds in the trunk and got pulled over. He did a year in jail for that. He would write me letters all the time.

Were you mad at him for going to jail?

I wasn't mad because he was in jail; I was mad because he wasn't here.

Did he encourage you to sell weed, too?

Basically, yeah. I remember when I was 14 my dad was living in New Mexico. I was talking with him on the phone, and I told him I'm trying to get a summer job. He was like, "You can go see your uncle and work at the gate in Brooklyn." I didn't even know what the fuck that was. I went to go see my uncle, and it was basically a weed gate in Clinton Hill that I would have worked behind.

What's a gate?

That's what they call that shit, that's an old-school term for a trap house. I would have stood behind bulletproof glass selling weed. [Laughs.]

Would you have been paid by the hour?

I didn't ask. I was like, "I'm not fucking with that." At that time I was boosting and shit, and I would make money really quickly. My father also used to boost; he'd just be doing it in front of me and as a kid I would watch and learn.

What were your favorite things to boost?

All types of clothes. My father used to steal mad Polo shit—so funny. I got into that when I was a teenager, when I was down with the Lo-Lifes and shit. We'd fucking go out and steal shit every day. That shit used to be fun. [Laughs.] We'd go out in teams. I don't even know how we would come off with shit, ten young-ass kids wearing bright-ass colors and giant book bags stealing shit. I don't even get it. [Laughs.]

So you didn't want to work behind the gate?

Nah, I just didn't want to do that shit. I'm from Uptown; I didn't like Brooklyn. I still really don't.

Why not?

It's like an Uptown Manhattan kind of thing. I don't want to come all the way out here and deal with these people. You know how neighborhoods change and people are just different from neighborhood to neighborhood, I'm just like, "The fuck out of here." If I had started working there I would be a whole different type of drug dealer. [Laughs.] I'm not a street dealer who sells drugs on corners. I only did that once. I took a shift on a coke block and did some packs.

A pack?

They give you 100 $20-bags of coke and you sell those off. I forgot how much you get off that shit, maybe like $50–$60 per pack. I did like five packs.

You'd only earn 50¢ for selling a $20-bag of coke?!

But people don't buy one; like, nobody comes to buy one. You're selling 10-15 at a time like all day.

That's still terrible pay.

Yeah, it's bad. [Laughs.]

And the consequences are gnarly.

Yeah, when you're a street-level dealer, that's the type of shit you get. It depends on the block that you're on. When I was there doing that shit, the crack packs used to be $60-worth. You made $10 off each pack, but you'd sell so many of them shits. If the shift was four hours, you'd make $1,000. [Laughs.]

That's so many transactions. So how did you get hooked up working this block?

I grew up on this block and knew all these dudes who did all this shit. I'm like, "I'm broke, I need to do a pack." I did some packs, and I actually served a fiend right in front of this dude I grew up with who became a fucking DT! I was like, holy shit! He came up to me later that day and I just apologized.

While you were still working?

Nah, after I got off. He was talking to me and was like, "What the fuck are you doing over here? You shouldn't even be doing that shit." I was like, "Yeah, you're right," and I just apologized. I never sold drugs on the corner again. I can't fuck with that, that shit is ridiculous. It's not enough money either. There are certain places where you can make money, but if you make $1,000 in four hours, you'll spend that in two fucking hours. You'll just think, "Oh, I can make another grand tomorrow." Then you get locked up and you have no bail money or lawyer money but mad clothes and sneakers. [Laughs.] That is the stupidest shit ever.

That's what happened to friends you were with?

Mhm, and then when I was about 17–18, all my friends who I used to go boosting with got into the weed game and were either working for, or operating, delivery services, and they put me onto that. First, though, I wasn't even working for a service—I used to rob the runners! That was the shit! [Cackles hysterically.] That was the best shit ever!

Oh. How many runners did you rob?

Yo, so many. I used to do this shit every day. Every single day, seven days a week, I'd rob the serves.

How would you know who was arriving to sell weed?

There were different ways we would come up on the serves' phone numbers. My friends knew a lot of these young rich kids and they gave us the phone numbers they'd call. We'd call them to buildings on the Upper East Side, like deep on the Upper East Side where they'd just assume there's going to be money. Like East End Avenue, York Avenue, and all that shit. Or we'd catch people on Fifth Ave and 84th Street. Runners would come through there with extra work, like, mad drugs, 'cause they figured they were gonna do a big deal.

So how did you get them?

First we'd check out a building. A lot of those places would have doormen and shit, so you got to find a place with no doorman, and a vestibule where you can open the first door but the second one is locked and there's no camera. Those are always the best. You find those and make sure there's not too much traffic coming in and out. This is like when most services would work from 12–12, so you'd call at like 11:50. [Laughs.] You'd just get 'em! That shit is funny. We would just do that shit with no guns all the time. There were times that we did it with guns with no bullets, or guns with no firing pins, just in case you got bagged up, you wouldn't go to jail for the gun. My favorite shit, I had a little hammerhead I used to stick in people's backs. They'd feel the cold metal and be terrified. [Laughs.]

Did these robberies ever go wrong?

Some do try to fight back so we'd just beat them up. [Laughs.]

And if they didn't struggle?

It'd be just, "Give me your shit!" and we're out. We would take their beepers, too, and go sell to the last of their customers. [Laughs really hard.]

Oh my god. Wow.

We'd get beeps for the next few days. We'd call those custies and give them a new number—now they're our custies. [Laughs.]

Did you ever worry about going to serve them and there being someone from the previous serve waiting for you?

No, 'cause at that point, we were just getting these dudes every single day. You felt untouchable, like "Fuck 'em, what they gonna do?" This whole Downtown shit is very loose and completely different. These runners aren't gangsters and the people who own the serves aren't gangsters. There are few people who are. A lot of these kids, their serves get robbed and they're like, "Fuck, now I got to change my number." But some wouldn't. There were mad services that we would call repeatedly and rob.

Did you ever rob the same runner twice?

Yep. [Laughs.]

Was he like, "Oh shit, you again?"

[Laughs.] Nah, 'cause a lot of times we were wearing masks and shit. At that time the Bloods were a big deal, and we would rob people with red masks and red bandanas. [Laughs.] They would think they were getting robbed by them [Laughs.]

Robbing drug dealers never sounded so easy.

The thing is, it's a drug deal—a low-key thing. These dudes aren't going to come out the building screaming, "You robbed me for my drugs!" In fact, a lot of times we'd run up on these dudes and they would think they were getting *arrested*. I would throw people on walls and frisk them. Sometimes I'd go in someone's pocket and there's $2,000, and then another $100 in this one, and then I'd go in their nuts and there's like $3,000 in there. Sometimes we would zip-tie people and we would leave them. [Laughs.]

That's really sadistic. On a typical night how many would you rob?

We'd really just try to get one and be done in like half an hour. We didn't want to be doing that shit all day. At first, we were real cutthroat and took everything. I'd take his bike, his wallet, all his personal shit.

Why did you stop taking personal items?

I was just on some karma shit, 'cause I ended up getting robbed once when I was running—I'll tell that story in a minute. We would rob dudes; I would take people's wallets just to scare the shit out of them. Take their wallet, pull their ID out, "Yo, I know where you live." [Laughs.] But then I would just throw it in the mailbox like right after I left. [Laughs.] It's all mental shit so they don't bug out and start screaming and calling the police and shit like that.

So you did this with one other guy? You guys were close?

He was like my best friend in the world.

Would you guys go have fun after you robbed somebody?

Hell yeah. We would catch somebody, bounce, jump in a cab, go Uptown, split up the money, split up the work, and figure out what we were going to do with it. Is it enough to sell to these people's custies, or should we just smoke this shit? Then sometimes there just be mad cash and like four 50s left. There were a couple of times we robbed dudes and they had nothing. They had like two 50-bags and $100. Then you really want to rob them and take their watch and jewelry, and shit like that. You got to leave that though, 'cause if you come out the building and you only have two jars of weed, $100, and a fucking chain and a watch, that person can start screaming for the police. That actually happened.

I remember we called this service that was supposed to be popping. This kid shows up—he doesn't have a book bag on—but he's definitely the runner. I see him looking from the address to the building. I was like, "Yo, maybe he has coke since he doesn't have a bag." We run up on this dude, push him in the vestibule, fucking tie him up like he's getting locked up. Go in his pockets, motherfucker got $300 and two 50-bags, I was like, "What the fuck?" We searched him crazy, looking for everything, go in his nuts, nothing, going in his socks, take his shoes off, nothing. He does have, however, this crazy TAG Heuer watch, and my boy went crazy trying to get it off his wrist. He snapped his nail all the way down to the base trying to pop this shit off. [Laughs.] I was like, "Yo, leave the fucking watch." We're arguing front of the dude we're robbing. He's like, "Fuck that, I want his fucking watch."

What's the dude doing?

He's scared shitless because we have a fucking gun to his face. It had no firing pin and only one bullet for the pull-back action we'd do. [Laughs.] He's not saying a fucking word, he's quiet. I got a gun to his fucking head, boy is taking his fucking watch off and shit, he finally gets it off and we get out of the building. We go two blocks down and jump in a cab. We're in the cab, and I'm arguing with my boy, "You're a fucking idiot, why the fuck did you do that? You shouldn't have taken his fucking watch." We're stuck in traffic and this motherfucker comes screaming down the block and comes to the cab and starts beating on the window, "Gimme my watch! Gimme my watch! My grandmother gave me that watch!" [Laughs.] I'm sitting in the fucking car, it's summertime and I have a hoodie on and a gun in the pocket, and I say to my friend, "You fucking asshole, give him the fucking watch." He's like, "No, no, I'm not giving him shit." This motherfucker is reaching in the window, crying, "Gimme my watch!" The cab driver is like, "What's going on? Get out of my cab!" I was like, "Just drive, drive, drive." I threw $100 at the cab driver, like, "Just take us Uptown." He's like, "No, you robbed that guy, get out of my cab." I was like, "Give him that fucking watch you idiot!" So he gives him the watch back.

No, he just takes his watch and burns down the street. Now the cab driver has locked us in the cab. I was like "Yo, take us Uptown! You have to take us Uptown!" He's like, "Why'd you take the watch?" So we convinced the cab driver that the kid owed us money and we took his watch 'cause he didn't pay. That was a funny one, but I was so pissed off by that shit.

Nobody running around Downtown selling weed is going to have a fucking gun on them. If they do, they a maniac. It's just not worth the risk. If you only get caught with weed you'll be out tomorrow working again.

I'll be in jail for like two, three weeks. 'Cause then I tell my lawyer, "Yo, have them look at that gun, it's inoperable." A gun with no firing pin is a paperweight. You'll be locked up for a minute, don't get me wrong, you'll have a court case and you're gonna be in jail, but you're not going to jail for a year. If I'm caught with it in the midst of a robbery, they'll charge me for armed robbery. But like I said, nobody is going to report, "I just got robbed for my drugs."

I was 18 or 19. Shit was crazy, too, 'cause I played myself so hard. I had seen these dudes following me three fucking times.

Within a couple of hours. I was riding around doing my runs and shit, I saw these motherfuckers on 28th and Second Avenue. Then I saw them again on 14th and Sixth. Then I see them again right by the Brooklyn Bridge on this really shady, dirty-ass fucking block! I was like, "The fuck?" It was two Puerto Rican dudes on motorcycles. I was like, "These motherfuckers ain't following me. They better not be following me!" I was all up in my head with this gangster shit. [Laughs.] I was down there selling to this Asian dude that I fucking hated with a passion 'cause he would only do a 50 and he'd always be a dollar short. So I flipped on him. This motherfucker gave me four quarters and I was like [laughs], "I don't want that shit!" and I threw it back at him and left. As I'm coming into the vestibule, those two fucking Puerto Rican motherfuckers put a knife to my face, another one to my throat.

Yikes.

They were like, "Whose serve is this? Whose serve is this?" As soon as I hear that I was thinking, "These are some bitch-ass niggas, why are you even asking whose serve this is if you're already robbing me?" I was like, "This is [serve name redacted] shit, you don't want to fuck with it." He's like, "What? Uh, uh, just give us the work!" and didn't even take my money. They gave me my bag back, gave me my keys, and all my shit. I'm thinking, "Oh, you fucking faggots. Either I know these people, or they know my peoples, they know my crew and shit and they realize they're fucking up." They tell me, "Just tell them you didn't see no faces, tell them we had masks on, and tell them we just took the work," and then they biked off. I was kind of confused as to what happened right there. I mean, you can't rob the robber! [Laughs.] That shit ain't right! I leave the building and I call my man that I was working for, he comes through on the motorcycle and I jump on the back and we ride around looking for these motherfuckers. He's like, "Yo, which way did they go? Did they get on the bridge?" I was like, "Nah, they actually started going Uptown." We didn't find them. I was so pissed; my boy that I was working for was like, "Oh, you don't have to worry about paying me for that shit." I was like, "Nah," it was like a half-onion so I just gave him the money. I was like, "That's my fault 'cause I saw these motherfuckers following me, I'll take that L."

The loss.

Yeah, I don't like owing someone money, even though I owe

my current boss money. [Laughs.] Anyhow, I remember like a month later we were at this huge, stupid club in Queens, like Metronome or some shit. We were out there chilling when I smelled the weed I had been robbed for. I looked over and there were those Puerto Rican motherfuckers, smoking my weed! I recognized them and their crew as these idiots from the low-income part of Roosevelt Island. We had had an ongoing thing with them.

Wait, really? You could identify your weed in a club by its scent?

The shit that we had at that point was really bomb and no one else had it. I knew that was *the* weed.

It's a month later. How do they still have your weed?

They obviously hadn't smoked it all yet. My boy was trying to talk me out of shit. I was like, "Nah B, these motherfuckers had knives to my neck, I was shook! I had to pay money for that shit." He's like, "Not now, not now." I was like, "Yeah, right now! This shit has to happen, I'm fucking somebody up." We had bottle service so I grabbed one and cracked one of the Puerto Ricans in the head with that shit, and then we all just started fighting. My crew was about 40 people. They were like 10.

You fought on the dance floor?

In the table section, whatever VIP bullshit. These Roosevelt Island kids thought they were gangsters but they were fucking faggots. That shit is just so funny to me, I don't understand people.

Why were they faggots, per se?

They were herbs. If you came back at them, if you punched one of those dudes in the face, they gonna back down, they not gonna fight you. Or they'll come with a gun—that shit is soft. I say, fight me, I'll fight you, if I lose, I don't give a fuck. Anyway, these dudes were mad soft and we fucked them up that night. I felt better about that shit.

Are these stories that you've shared with your dad?

Nah, not all of this shit. I don't speak to my father too often. My father was living in New Mexico when all this shit was happening.

If you told your father about all this how do you think he would have reacted?

He would probably laugh. [Cackles.]

DARYL

29, East Williamsburg

How long have you worked as a messenger?

About eight years now. I've worked for three companies in New York so far—two at the moment. One is a courier company and the other is a "serve," a service that delivers weed. I mean, we sell edibles and stuff, too, but it's mainly weed. Some friends who are also bike messengers hooked me up with this job.

Is this the "courier underworld"?

Yeah, I think so, but it also doesn't have much to do with being an actual bike messenger. It's just that you use your bike to get around while you sell weed. It's not so time-sensitive that you need to have something somewhere by 5 p.m. and there's no ifs, ands, or buts. With a serve you have to be somewhere within 30–45 minutes as a courtesy. Really, what you're doing for these customers is a favor.

Did you have any hesitation getting into that line of work?

Just before I got into it, one of my friends got popped—arrested. That outcome was already in the back of my head, so at first I was hesitant and it was stressful. You just have to constantly look over your back and keep an eye on what's going on around you. You can't be carefree.

What kind of things did you have to look out for?

I pay attention to the cars on the street. Undercovers have certain kinds of cars; the main ones are the older Crown Victorias. They also use Ford Fusions, and Nissan Altimas. You also look for blacked-out windows and any antennas poking out in the back. I see these cars all the time.

What precautions do you take?

If I see them on an avenue I'll take note, but I won't be that concerned. Sometimes I might slow down a tad and let them get ahead of me; that way I can keep an eye on them without having to look over my shoulder. But when they're parked on a street, or if they're rolling real slow with the windows down, lookin', that's when I get very careful.

If you're on an avenue with an unmarked car around you, do you treat red lights any differently?

It depends. If there's a bunch of other cyclists and there are no cars coming, I'll go through the light with them. But if I'm the only one on the street, I'll wait for the green.

Have you ever been followed?

Yeah, I've been followed a couple of times. It was stressful, very stressful. Once I left a walk-up in the East 80s, by Third Avenue, when an unmarked car rolled by as I was getting to my bike, which I'd locked down the street. They pulled over and one of the plainclothes got out of the passenger seat and looked directly at me. I looked at him, too. I knew if I didn't start riding, he was going to come start asking me questions. I went down an avenue the wrong way and left the city.

Why did you lock your bike down the street? Is that a measure of precaution?

Yeah. It gives you a chance to take in your surroundings and see what's going on. It just looks less suspect if you leave a building and walk down the street instead of walking directly to the bike you locked right in front. That looks like you're delivering something. When I left the city that day, I called my phone guy, the dispatcher, and told him they definitely spotted me. He just told me to get out of there.

They weren't upset with you?

No, they're pretty good with that kind of stuff. They may call me later just to check that everything is OK.

What happens if the cops nab you?

There's an understanding: I don't say anything and I get let out. I've had friends who've gotten picked up and they've gotten their money and their bikes back. Other times they don't get the money back at all. I don't think the charges ever stick.

Does your serve have a lawyer on retainer?

They say they do, whether or not that's true, I don't know.

Did lawyers show up for your coworkers?

I don't think anybody showed up. I think they say that they have a lawyer to put you at ease, but their lawyers are for the people upstairs; I don't think it has anything to do with the runners.

How much do you make in a day working for the serve?

It's commission-based.

What's the worst, average, and record best you've done in a day?

The lowest I've ever made is probably $20 for selling $80-worth. It was so slow I was just sitting around, like, "Can I go home?"

On average I can probably make around $200–250 per day. The most I made is around $600.

What did you do after you were done with work that day?

I went out with my friends and we wilded out. We went out to the bar, partied, bought drinks for our friends. I don't know, you make so much money, you feel bad just keeping it all to yourself. They're my friends, why not? I had fun. It's definitely a good feeling when you go home and you look at that cash in your hand.

What's the most you've spent at the bar after a night of making a lot of money selling weed on a bike?

Probably $200. My friends and I would all thrown down on coke at the bar.

Like the scenario where the coke dealer goes to the bathroom and sells to a bunch of people at once?

Yeah, like that. Those are long nights man, long nights.

The following day is longer.

Yeah.

After a night like that would you rather work on the bike or have a day off?

As much as it would suck for it to happen, it's probably best for you to get on the bike and work it out of your system. If you had a late night—say you went to bed around 9 or 10 a.m.—you'll sleep until noon, 12:30. When you wake up you're definitively still drunk, and the last bit of coke is still kicking through you. When you get on your bike, the first two hours you drag ass—it hurts. But after that, once you get something to eat and you get a good sprint in the city, you feel like a million bucks.

Do you smoke weed?

No, I don't.

You're the weed dealer who doesn't smoke; you're *that* guy.

Yeah, everybody makes fun of me for it. I don't like how it makes me feel paranoid and really introverted. I just don't do it, that's all.

What do you think of your customers?

I don't care about these people I go to; I see them as dollar bills.

You don't see them as unique individuals?

There are some you go to all the time and you build a little bit of a relationship, but it's more that it's a drug dealer relationship. It's like, "Hey, what's going on, we're friends because I'm giving you what you need." Then there's the creepy people, and the odd people—there's not just one kind of person that smokes weed. Everybody smokes: grandmas, grandpas, moms, dads, obviously young kids, artists, business kids, people who work at Fortune 500 companies.

What buildings do you sell in?

All kinds of buildings, Trump towers, high-rises. One Central Park West is pretty cool. It's just fancy inside, and all the apartments are completely over the top. The nice thing about the job is you get a peek into their lifestyle and how they live. Some people are extremely tidy and neat. Others might live in a really nice, doorman building but their apartment is just a dump with rotting food piled up everywhere.

But they have a gorgeous harbor view. Has your mode of dress changed since you worked for this service?

Oh yeah. When I first started, I definitely dressed like a bike messenger. When I had that run-in on the Upper East Side, I was riding home and thinking, "I got profiled." I realized, "What is a bike messenger doing working at 8 p.m. on a Saturday?" The next day I wasn't working so I just went out and bought a bunch of button-downs, chinos, and a pair of Clarks.

Business casual, like an everyday commuter.

Everyday bike commuter, and when I'm off the bike, I'm dressed like I live on the Upper East Side.

Did you change up your bike, too?

I haven't changed it yet, but I just put a down payment on another bike that I'm going to use while working for the service.

What does that bike look like?

It's single speed and has breaks. I'm gonna put full fenders on it.

Is it gonna bum you out that you're not going to use your preferred messenger bike?

No, not at all. When I'm working at the service, I don't ever feel pressured to ride really fast. I frown upon zipping from place to place; otherwise, I might raise suspicion.

Does it mess with your bike messenger ego to not look the part, to not ride the part?

At first it bugged me because when I changed my look I looked like a student or somebody maybe that just got out of the office. I've been a bike messenger for seven years and these messenger kids are looking at me like I just found a track bike. I've actually had kids ride beside me and scoff.

Haha!

Yeah, just give me the stink eye because I look like a preppy kid. Never mind that when I started bike messengering they were still in middle school. But now I don't think about it anymore, I don't even care. It's actually kind of nice to dress up; I feel nicer about myself.

Why did you do this interview?

I guess I didn't want to withhold my knowledge from other people who do what I do. If I see [another weed courier] doing something wrong, or being obvious, I let them know. For example, my friend told me my dressing like a messenger was raising a red flag, and that I should start wearing Polo shirts, comb my hair, and to trade the messenger bag for an everyday book bag. If we share our knowledge it will make us better. It helps everybody.

Anything you want to add? "Fuck the police," perhaps?

Nah, I'm not like that.

No "Fuck the police"?

They're doing their job. I don't wish harm on anyone.

GORDON

30, Chelsea

So you work at this textile company, and you sell what on the side?

At the moment I decided it would be a good idea to try hustling some molly, because it seemed like people up here in the scene had a noticeable interest in feeling good, being able to still drink, being at a party….

I've heard a lot of buzz about molly in the past year or two, particularly in rap music. Where do you get this stuff?

I know a dude domestically who gets it from Holland, so he gets good shit; apparently it's in the 80th-percentile of pure MDMA. I got two different kinds from him at the moment. There's an amber-colored one that everyone thinks is speedier; you do it and you're really up, moving around, and ready to do shit. Then I have one that's more beige. It still hits you and comes on strong, but people say they prefer it because it's a smoother kind of good feeling.

Yeah, I've done them both. Molly comes in crystals and you can get big chunks, or they can be tiny. I kind of leave it mostly intact because I think people like to see the product. The amber-crystals are very impressive looking, actually.

Probably a third of a gram, which is about the size of an old school pencil-tip eraser. Some people are gung-ho enough to crush it and snort it; I wouldn't personally want to because it would really burn your sinuses. I put it in these vegan gel caps. I measure doses out as a tenth of a gram. That's definitely a medium-sized dose, but it depends on its quality.

I talk to a few people in Williamsburg who go to parties every weekend and want to dance and get fucked up and shit. I haven't gone on much of a campaign of making it known or anything. Molly can be a pain in the ass to procure sometimes, so I haven't turned it into a full-scale, "this is what I'm doing" operation.

I wish I was making better money at my day job. I guess, yeah, probably. If the money was there. At this point in my life I need to move forward, I need to make money. Freedom is costly. But even if molly became a full-time thing I would keep a side job so my having money wouldn't be suspect.

I mean, yeah, in a sense. I was never necessarily looking to get into the fashion industry, it kind of fell into place like that. I have a general college degree in design. I'm furthering my skills in that aspect, building up a résumé of sorts, building up a portfolio of things I've done. This job is a stepping stone for something. I've worked there for a combined six or seven years. It's part of a greater ambition to be more hirable and shit.

Do you worry about drug dealing overcoming that legal ambition, or distracting you at least?

It might be a distraction, yeah, but it wouldn't stop me from doing what I want to do ultimately. I feel like other, different, stupider shit is more of a distraction to me than selling molly.

Like what?

Wasting time, playing video games, you know. Not using my time to the best of my ability. I should be at home drawing, designing things at all free hours of the day that I have, but I'm just dicking around usually, because I'm exhausted.

After you get out of work, do you go out to meet people to sell molly?

I have, but I usually go home, stock up, and then go back out and get rid of that shit.

When you're in midtown at 6 p.m. and you see the teeming seas of people leaving work, it's easy to assume they're all a bunch of corporate squares; not people who have molly in their pocket that they intend to sell.

That's very true.

Do you think selling drugs makes a square hip? Can it enhance the authenticity of their life?

No.

Rap music will argue with you.

Right, I agree fully. I think a lot of people *think* it would enhance your life, but I think it depends where you come from. If you came from a very sheltered existence where you didn't have a lot of excitement, I can see how selling drugs could add a level of complexity to your life and make it more interesting. But there are people who try to sell drugs who are just stupid. I know a kid who started buying coke from me back when I sold coke, and he ended up wilding out thinking he was gonna be a dealer, like for real, and he ended up selling a kilo of coke to the cops.

What measures have you taken that this molly hustle doesn't bite you in the ass?

I usually don't fuck with people that I don't know well. Mostly I deal with people that I've had a relationship with aside from hustling. If somebody comes up to me and isn't introduced and is like, "Yo, I heard you got drugs, what's up?" I'll tell them to go talk to someone else. I don't carry shit on me unless there's a pre-planned meeting. I would take even more precautions if I was moving pounds of molly, but I'm only dealing with ounces.

A couple of ounces would still land you in prison, huh?

That's still definitely a long prison sentence. But I'm not going out with a couple ounces.

Where do you get your ounces?

I actually get my shit delivered directly when it's time to re-up, so I don't have to worry about that anymore. I do know how it feels to go pick up ounces of coke; that's like the scariest ride that you'll take, driving home with three ounces in your car. That's not fun [laughs], that's not exhilarating. Fuck that.

How do you blend in?

I mean, I am an average, middle-class white dude; I look fairly boring. I don't have anything flashy. At the very worst, the police might think I'm smoking weed or I have a joint under my seat.

Being white helps you sell drugs.

Definitely, people are still classist, racist, and, judgmental in general. I mean, I'm very present of mind to not attract attention to myself, to the point of paranoia. I'll fuck with my phone just to look like everybody else that's walking around, because they're all fucking with their phones. All things equal, I'm still hoping and praying to not be harassed by the police.

MISS TOKE

22, Williamsburg

So…you're a drug dealer?

OK, so I just quit being a drug dealer maybe a month ago. I was phasing it out because I was like, "Well, this is stupid; I'm just going to buy a little less weed."

What was stupid?

I wasn't making any money. At the end of it I was just picking up an ounce, and then I would smoke/sell it, and I would go through it in a week. It was just helping me smoke for nothing.

Weren't you good at it?

I just didn't give a shit. It got to the point where I had no interest in pursuing it because it was no longer convenient. If I was working at my restaurant and my coworkers bought from me, or if I was at home and someone wanted to cop from me, that was fine. But, obviously, it's not lucrative. I still have friends who will be like, "Oh, can I come get a gram?" I don't even care, like, "Sure…I dunno, whatever."

When did you first get into selling drugs?

All my boyfriends have been potheads, even when I didn't really smoke at all. I would be like, "Wouldn't it be funny if I sold drugs? I don't smoke weed!" It would just be like, "hahaha," if I were selling it.

You never fell for the gangster allure of the whole trade?

Oh, yeah, I guess now that I think about it, sure. I was always a little girl who wished she was born a badass. Then when I went to college at Pratt I started smoking a lot of weed and hung out with this girl who lived across the hall from me in the dorms. She'd been selling weed all through high school and whatever else she could get her hands on, like shrooms. After the dorms we moved in together just across the street from Pratt, and she got back into it because all the students would just come over during lunch breaks. My friend and another girl operated this—

—Weed lounge.

Sure. I just lived there and smoked a lot of weed and did them favors, but they were the ones who put their money in and dealt with it all.

Didn't they worry about one of these kids getting busted with a dime bag and then ratting on them? I mean, especially if your girlfriends' ring is known among the student body and anyone can freely go in and buy?

Not anyone. Someone would have to be like, "Hey, so-and-so sent me." They would have to get our number from someone else. It was supposed to be a network of friends and if they were a stranger, it would be like—and especially if they were going to come over to the house—"Hey, who are you?" Also, the girls would take a lot of weed out with them and sell at parties. That was the easiest. Lunch breaks would be a series of people rolling through and picking up while we had friends hanging out anyway, smoking weed and chilling. There was always a roommate home at the apartment, and that's how I got into it: more and more they started relying on me, calling me like, "Hey, are you home? Someone wants to come through, blahblahblah."

How would you be compensated?

At first I was just paid in free weed. I smoked all the weed I wanted. I thought it was fun and exciting and "gangster" to go pick up a bunch of weed and do things with it.

How much would you guys pick up at a time?

Just a QP every time and fill up a big mason jar.

Would you have different varieties at a time?

No, no.

You wouldn't know the actual strain you were selling?

Sometimes. We really didn't care. It was like, "Let's just smoke it and see if it's good or not." It wasn't like, "Come into my office and scope out my selection," all *Pulp Fiction*-style.

So in a month, how much were your two roommates making?

I don't know because they wouldn't tell us but maybe they were paying their rent with it. They would each make up to $300–$400 a batch depending how much of it we didn't smoke, and we'd probably go through a batch every week or two weeks. Oh, and I also sold Adderall because one of my roommates was over-prescribed so she would sell it to students during finals. They would pick it up when they came for weed.

Who did your friends buy their quarter-pounds from?

They had some city friends who did a lot of drugs. At the time they were living in Greenpoint. It's not that hard to find sellers.

Were there other people on campus who were selling weed?

Yeah, definitely, and we were friends with some of them.

Any hard feelings?

No, because there weren't that many of them. Actually there was a security guard at Pratt who used to sell weed to the freshmen—he'd visit your dorm room. But Pratt has cleaned up their system so much since those days. There wasn't much competition among dealers because there were enough students. Most of the potheads were friends and they thought it was cool that they were all drug dealers. I mean, it's an art school full of white kids; nobody cares.

Yeah, but there was still money at stake.

It's small-time shit: kids buying weed. [The cops] never really paid attention. The only way I could have gotten busted was in a stop and frisk. I think the reason my friends and I feel less nervous is because we're women. Little, white—well, one friend is Asian—girls. Cops smile at us. They're nice to me.

When did you start earning money?

After a while they started paying me because I was working all the time and doing deliveries here and there.

I was going to ask if you did house calls.

If it was in the neighborhood and they were friends, then yeah. Not only would my roommates let me smoke for free which had been going on for a while but they started giving me money. It wasn't a lot. Then one of the girls in our apartment moved back to the West Coast, and the other girl didn't want to do this alone, so she asked me to be her partner. I was like, "Yeah, sure." I only did that for a few months, and that is when I made actual money. But school let out and I was only making $200 a [re-up], which is nice, but it's not a business. We would sit on a lot of it and then smoke it all and not make any money. That is what was happening in the end: we would have this pound of weed, lazily sell it, and smoke a lot of it. We'd be smoking for

43

free but not making any profit.

How much weed would you girls smoke if you were going to have a night in?

Ooh, my god! See, that's why I kept selling—I'm the biggest pothead you know. I make weed art. I make bong prints. It was in my senior thesis at Pratt. I had an art installation that was about drugs and alcohol, influences and mind-altering-whatever. So I included some fake coke made of baking soda. My retarded drug friend said it needed to look more crystaly, so we added salt.

What grade did you get?

I don't know. I don't know if you even really get a grade. You just pass, basically. They liked it because I spent time on it. You're allowed to make what you want as long as you make it nice. But people made a lot of fun of me.

Did it bother you?

Yes. I remember I made a pamphlet about stoner prejudice. It has George Washington on the front. He used to grow weed!

Right, but for hemp.

Yeah, but so did Thomas Jefferson.

It's a great textile.

It is! And apparently they smoked it, too—whether that's true or not, I don't really care. But the pamphlet was about how there are a lot of different potheads, and we are not all just people who sit on the couch and—

—Make stoner art.

I do! That's true. Stereotype me, that's fine. I'm just saying there are doctors and lawyers and businessmen who smoke weed. My father has been a stoner his entire adult life and he's a businessman in Silicon Valley and he is on his shit 24/7, but he smokes weed because he likes it.

Does your dad know about your weed lounge in college?

Yeah. My dad and I became better friends once we started smoking weed with each other when I was 19.

Did he know you were selling weed out of your house?

Not until he came to visit and he saw our big jar of weed, a fucking scale, and baggies around. He caught on, although he never really asked.

He wasn't mad?

No, he was like, "Oh, wow, look at this big ol' thing! Cool, awesome!" Obviously he doesn't want me to get arrested and go to jail for something as stupid as selling weed—and if we had a talk about it I know that's exactly what he would say. But he smoked bongs with us and when he comes to visit we give him little baggies and set him up in his hotel room.

My dad said he would smoke a joint with me after he retires. He hasn't smoked since he was in college.

Oh, that's so cute! I kind of want to be an animal cop someday, but I'm like, fuck, they're going to drug-test me; it's a government job. So this means I need to move somewhere that has legal weed.

So when did you call it a wrap with the lounge?

When my roommate and I finally admitted there was no more point to selling weed. We were over it. We had other things we wanted to do with our time. Then I started picking up from my manager at my restaurant job—and he's just a white dad who doesn't mind buying extra for everyone else—and I would get a half-ounce or something. But then enough people asked me that I decided to just pick up a whole ounce and make my money back. I would casually carry around three grams with me, and I'd flip 'em out to whoever came around. I stopped that when I stopped my restaurant job, and now I have a bike messenger guy who delivers weed to my house—he's my first drug dealer in New York.

45

Do you enjoy exploiting people's ideas of a "young, little white girl"?

Yeah, definitely. I feel like it's a Napoleon complex-thing of maybe wanting to have been born big and tough like a big-man, some hood dude—just a badass. I used to be really not down with being a tiny white girl from California.

What, you felt like a wimp?

Yeah, I guess so, like a wimp or just boring and regular. I can't be badass with hands like these! I definitely got a lot of pleasure passing by cops—of course I get nervous and like, "Fuck, fuck, fuck!" But then I realize they just think I'm some cute, li'l fuckin' white girl in leather shoe-boots and a plaid coat. They don't even know. I think women make good criminals because we're just not suspect—period. And we can talk our way out of things and people believe us. It's really easy to play dumb as a girl.

BILLY

19, Prospect Heights

Have you ever been stopped by the cops?

Yeah. The only times I've been stopped by the cops is when I'm coming home real late at night. I just show them my ID and they're like, "Oh, OK. Go on."

Why would showing them your ID get you out of a stop?

I have a military ID. Because my dad was in the military, I get to carry one until I'm 24.

You're saying the NYPD gives special consideration to people affiliated with the service?

Yeah. Of course. [Scoffs.] Are you serious?

Did you have anything on you?

Yeah, I just had random Percocets, I don't even know what Percocet does.

You never tried one?

No.

You know they're downers, right?

I don't know.

[Laughs.] I guess Percocet sells itself.

When I got into drug dealing I knew nothing about drugs. I never did drugs, and I'm not a particular fan of people who do drugs. I got into drug dealing in the 11th grade when I got into a fight the day the *Daily News* was at my school doing an article about it. The principal flipped shit and gave me a stupid suspension. The reporter actually mentioned the fight in the article.

[Laughs.]

To be fair, the article about my school was really nice. I got sent to this alternative learning center with all these degenerates [laughs], who were in and out of jail. This dude told me he could get me an ounce of kush for $400. I had no clue what that meant. [Laughs.] What he gave me was a Ziplock bag of literal dust.

Was it brown in color?

That was it, and I had no clue what weed was supposed to look like.

Wait, so you bought it?

Yeah.

How did you have $400 to invest?

I worked at Best Buy. At that point I had no clue how to sell anything; I didn't do any Internet.

Didn't visit a drug dealer forum?

I went back to my original school, and how I sold it was like, "Just take some and give me some money."

How much money would you get for a handful?

Kids at my school were dumb, so they would give me like $30. I made my money back and a $100 profit. I was like, "Maybe I should do this more."

But you got ripped off in the first place.

Yeah, but the guy made it up to me by giving me 50 ecstasy pills for $50.

Are you sure it wasn't aspirin?

I think it was; I was new!

[Laughs.] But you were selling it and didn't have any complaints?

I think kids liked *pretending* to use drugs.

So how much did you sell these E pills for?

I heard they sell 'em for $15 apiece, so that's how much I sold them for.

Did you sell them to your friends?

My friends don't really do drugs. I would just walk up to random people on the street in the middle of the day, like, "Hey, I have drugs. I don't look that shady; want to buy some?"

Kids your age?

No, just random people. I'd go by NYU and just stand around trying not to look suspect. At one point I actually went to 14th Street and tried to do it. Don't go to 14th Street and try to sell drugs, 'cause the vagrants over there kind of have a hold on it. They don't like when people go over there and try to sell drugs—at all.

How do you suss out a plainclothes cop?

'Cause it's obvious as hell to tell a cop from a normal person; they *look* like they want to buy drugs.

Any brushes with a plainclothes cop?

Yeah, one once asked me if I had any weed and I told him no, that I didn't do that. Then he went over and asked my friend and he was like, "Yeah, sure, I'll sell you some." Then a minute later four cop cars came in and the cop grabbed him and pushed him against the wall. I just walked away casually.

What did the cop look like?

White, had a beard. He was wearing some Adidas—looked pretty regular. But who walks up to someone and asks if they sell weed? Well, that actually happens a lot on 34th Street, in front of the Empire State Building. When I'm camping out there [in a sneaker line], a lot of Upper West Side kids come up to me and ask if I'm selling drugs.

Does it bother you that they're probably racially profiling you?

Well, I mean, if a black guy is in a sneaker line buying sneakers that cost $160, yeah, he's probably selling drugs.

That's racist!

No it's not. He most likely sells drugs.

Couldn't he just be a rich kid?

Last time I checked, rich kids don't buy $175 Jordans.

You don't talk to the Asians in these sneaker lines?

Oh, yeah.

Come on.

That's different—they're Asian.

What does that mean?

They always buy the newest kicks that come out. I don't think they sell drugs, but they must have some kind of hustle.

So you sold all these E pills, what kind of a profit did you turn out?

I made a huge profit, I only paid $50 for the E pills, and I sold them for $15 apiece. I gave a few of them away for free, but I had a lot of money from them. I actually went back to the guy to get some more. I was making way more money off that than I was off weed dust. Now I sell Percs and X—that's it.

Before this interview I thought you worked a coke block.

I want to sell coke so badly, it's not even funny. It's so easy to make money off cocaine. I can't [afford] to get into it.

Could you just start small with $5,000 of coke and build up a nest egg?

I don't really want to deal with all that. I know a few people who do it who I could sell to, but not that many that I can push that kind of volume. I try to get all my friends in on it but they don't want to do it. Most of them sell weed but there's no money in weed compared to other drugs.

So how many pills do you sell a week?

A week? Believe it or not, I actually just sold out today. I'd say 70 pills a week.

So how much money is that, on average?

It's a lot, say, over a G. I beat my kids at school over the head with pills. "Oh, you want a Percocet? That's $25." [Laughs.] You know that's like rape for a Percocet, right?

Honestly, I don't buy pills, I don't know rates.

It's a lot, you could get Percocet for like $5.

If someone wants something, do they call you on your disposable phone?

No, they call me on my regular phone.

How do they let you know whether they want this or that?

At first when I did it, this girl—I'm not going to say her name—she calls me and she's like, "Yo, let me get a dupper."

A "dupper"?

I'm like, "What the fuck is that?" [Laughs.] Just say what you want, I doubt any cops are listening to my conversations.

With the Patriot Act, the government can—

Yeah, well, I don't think they are saying, "Oh, let's go after that college kid who seems kind of suspect." I feel like there's this unnecessary paranoia that hustlers have—no reason for it. I mean, I've never been locked up, so maybe that's it. Maybe if I had been locked up, I would be more cautious.

Do you appreciate rap music more now that you sell drugs?

Not really, they are rappin' how much money they are making off of this; I'm making no money off of this. I mean, I do well enough to buy Supreme [laughs], that's about it. I can't go out and buy a car.

You could.

I mean, I have enough savings, I have enough savings to buy a '95 Accord.

So you got like $3,000 saved?

Like $3,500, [laughs] that's it.

So are you serious about your ambition to sell coke?

Yeah, pretty serious, I really want to be able to. I feel like I'll be making more money, just to be able to afford stuff.

Like what?

You know, expensive stuff, like Givenchy, Alexander McQueen for my girlfriend.

And she would like you more?

No, she already likes me, I'm an amazing person, I'd just be cooler because of that. Nobody dates a drug dealer and wants to settle for less.

You could sniff out a coke serve and see if they will hire you.

Yeah, I know some. I know a lot of people. I want to do it independently and make my own little crew, and have my own come up.

If you run the serv, you'll have to have a really good lawyer on retainer.

I actually have a lawyer.

Really?

That's just because I get in trouble with the law, but I never get in trouble for hustling, ever. I get in trouble for other things.

Like what?

Being in a park after dark. You'd think the cops would stop and search me, but they never do. I just show them my ID and they give me a summons. Reason why I got a lawyer is because every time I get a summons, I go to court and the city-appointed one would screw me over and be like, "Just plead guilty and pay the ticket."

I know, they have too many cases.

I'm like, "I just paid four $300 tickets, I'm not paying any more. I might as well get a lawyer." Also, I've had legal cases, for stuff. I have a pretty good criminal lawyer.

That's pretty proactive for a teenager to go seek out a lawyer. Do your friends view you differently since you became a drug dealer?

Yeah, 'cause they all assume I have this amazing amount of money. I blame rap music, like "Oh, watch me count my stack."

What do you study in college?

Teacher education.

So you want to be a high school teacher?

Yes.

Does part-time drug dealing clash with that?

I mean, if I get caught, that dream is pretty much over.

Yeah, you're right; you could probably never get a job with kids.

You really couldn't. Well, you can, but at some shitty inner-city school where the kids will stab you. Yeah, for any professional teaching career, the dream would be gone, but I guess I'm willing to take that risk.

Just for spending money?

True.

How much do you make a month? $2,000?

[Laughs.] It's a bit less than that.

Really?

Yeah. If I could clear $2,000, it's an amazing month. I mean, yeah, I pull in like a G in profit, actual profit.

This doesn't seem at all worth the risk.

What should I do, go back to working at Target? No, no, I can't do that. I like Target actually, but I'm not going back.

Have you ever been robbed?

Yes, and guess where at? Williamsburg. I was already pissed that I had to take the L train, because you have the worst gentrifiers, then after a point comes dangerous, dangerous hood people. I got off at Bedford and four guys ran up and grabbed me.

Right at Bedford and North 7th Street?

Yeah, I got robbed in broad daylight. Nobody called the cops. These guys grabbed my money—I had like a low wallet, only $75, but it was in low denominations, so it felt like something. They didn't even take the really good bud I had on me. No. I just stood there in disbelief for like half an hour.

Who were these guys?

I didn't know; people contact me out of the blue all the time.

That's dangerous.

I'm always scared that someone is going to set me up, 'cause someone did that in the past, in high school. Someone got caught with a little bit of weed, and they ratted me out. The cops thought I had stuff on me at school, so they pulled me out of class and searched me. I got a summons; I don't know what it was for. Ever since then I've been scared that someone is going to snitch on me.

Isn't that what the Stop-Snitching movement is about, this kind of snitching?

I respect that, I don't respect when someone innocent gets shot and nobody wants to come forward and say who did it. I respect a man like that, but yeah, you should otherwise probably stop snitching.

You should just take the lump.

Take the L, if you would.

BRIAN

24, Lower East Side

So where does this start?

It starts with my moving from Long Island to Orlando, Florida.
I wasn't getting along with my immediate family so I moved in
with my grandpa and I started going to college. Then I met this
guy at school. He pulls up in a Benz and he's smoking some
nice piff.

Some nice what?

Some nice weed. I had another group of friends that wanted
me to pick up for them, so that's how I started hanging out with
these guys. I could tell they were up to something. I said to the
boss-kid, "Listen, if you ever need me to do something, give
me a call." About a week later he calls at nine in the morning.
He tells me to meet them for breakfast because there would be

$1,000 waiting for me. I go there and he gives me the money. He says there would be another $5,000 waiting for me at the end of the day if I went along with them.

What did you do?

We robbed a coke dealer's house.

Oh.

That was what they would do. Once a month we'd rob a drug dealer and then we would go down to Miami for 30 days and live it up. Then we would come back up and rob somebody else and go back down.

How would you guys know whom to target?

The boss-kid, his uncle was a big coke dealer. He would sell coke to people, tell us where they went, and we'd rob them and sell it back to him.

Were there things you would or wouldn't do?

At the time I was willing to do whatever I had to.

Why?

For acceptance into the crew. I didn't have to pass through a gang-initiation where you have to go to a shopping mall and slash some person's face or something; I had to successfully carry out a job.

Tell me about this first robbery.

We're sitting outside of a kid's house all day, snorting our guy's uncle's coke until the kid finally leaves his house and a car outside follows him. We go break a window but it turns out to be his neighbor. We break into the right house. We had been instructed to go take drugs and money but to not touch any guns—and there are guns everywhere. We go upstairs to the closet, take the shoeboxes, and get back into the car. We drive down the street and the boss-kid gets into another car and we take two different ways back to the house. We get home and realize we have two and a half bricks of cocaine, about $80,000 in cash, $50,000 in pills—just tons and tons of shit. We bring the drugs back to Miami and sell them to this kid's uncle and get cashed out. With that money the crew bought a boat, a Range Rover—we had money out the ass. We would buy these things but the uncle would register them in his name.

You guys were all pretty young.

Oh, yeah. I was 18, 19, 20.

Did your crew have a name?

No. Not then.

How often would you guys hang out?

Oh, all day, every day. Once you're doing shit like that, you have so much heat on you, you have to be with your boys all the time. Always with a gun—or a few.

Did you grandfather know what you were up to?

He had an idea. I mean, I stopped living with him because I was making so much money I started living with my boys.

Wait, so what happened to that first coke dealer you robbed?

So it turns out the neighbor lady called the cops about the attempted break-in. The cops came, walked around her house and see her neighbor's broken window as well. They see all the guns he has lying around, so they arrest the kid. They search the house they find another ten bricks of cocaine under the floor. That kid is now in jail for ten, 15 years.

This is out of a movie.

Yeah. So we would do a lick like that and go live on the rooftop at the Fontainebleau—it's the nicest hotel in Miami—for 20, 30 days. There's a club in there and we would go to the beach every day. Then at night we would switch off dropping $5,000, $10,000 at the door of a club, and go in on bottles and everything. These were just crazy, fun times. I worked with these guys for a minute; then I left that life down there after I went on a 36-day ecstasy binge—that was ten pills a day, which is a lot—but in Miami you can do that because clubs literally never close. [Chuckles.] I decided it was enough, and I came home.

After all that E you must have wanted to kill yourself.

Exactly, yeah. I literally did. I had never been so depleted—and I have done a lot of shit. [Pauses.] It was crazy. By this point there was a lot of heat on our crew, so I came back to New York and found an apartment in the Lower East Side and paid for it in cash. I actually enrolled in a trade school and became an electrician. Meanwhile, my crew robbed a pharmacy warehouse of 500,000 Xanax.

What does that look like?

That was like a pallet of 5,000 cases of Xanax. It was a *crate*. My being from New York, I had connections at schools like Syracuse, Albany, Buffalo, Binghamton, even Arizona: drug schools. Some schools could take 20,000 pills every week. It was a lot. My Florida crew would send me 20,000–30,000 pills a week—50,000, depending on what I would order.

How did you ship? UPS?

At first, that's how it would come until we lost a few packages in the mail. Then they would bring them up by person to my apartment in the Lower East Side. People would come there and pick them up. I was working that nine-to-five and coming home to this side-hustle. I was making a lot of money.

What precautions would you take?

I would change shitty cell phones once a week. I would always move around, go on vacations—it was the life.

How long was this period?

The selling of Xanax went on for six months. They moved 200,000 elsewhere and I sold 200,000–300,000. [Laughs.]

Yeah, man, we did some big deals, like $75,000 off just one. We would average $20,000 a week.

So how did you come across people to do deals with?

I mean, there were consistent people. There was this one kid in Albany who would come down every Wednesday for 20,000 tablets. I had friends from high school who were then all going to those schools so I would work with them—I wasn't just sending this shit to anyone. And they had off-shore accounts. It was a matter of doing things under $10,000.

You would do this through legit bank accounts?

Yeah, you would do it under $10,000 and you would use Western Union or MoneyGram.

What was the most amount of stuff you ever had at your place at the same time?

In that apartment? A lot of guns: an assault rifle, two shotguns, two or three handguns. I had literal pillowcases filled with 20,000–30,000 Xanax, $70,000–$80,000 in cash. Pounds of weed. I mean, my apartment was a storehouse. It was where the stuff would come to and where it would be taken from.

Did you ever worry about getting robbed?

It never happened but I did worry—that's why I had a bunch of guns in my apartment. Whenever we had a deal, I would have a gun in my waistband. But I had a sandbag shotgun in case I got robbed. I didn't want a dead body on the floor—the sandbag would just knock them out.

There must have been times of terrible anxiety, though.

You know, I was so fucked up on drugs at the time it was a blur. I would take so many Xanax and smoke some weed, coke, whatever… I didn't even know what I was doing. After that I would get requests for 5,000 here or there but that wasn't nearly enough to supply the demand I had, so we just fell off with it.

What did you do with all your money?

I bought a Dodge Charger and a Kawasaki Ninja ZX-10R. I went to Jamaica three times, I got a Siberian Husky I named Joxie, and I did a lot of OxyContin. My friends would come over and I would take out pillowcases of Xanax and we'd each swallow a handful. I was using a lot of dope, like heroin. When you're living in the Lower East Side, it's easy to get mixed up in that shit. So now my car is gone and my friend has Joxie. It was fun while it lasted, but I'm thankful to still be alive—and not in prison. I don't have anything to show for it except the motorcycle, which I'm also selling; I actually got a phone call about it today.

Where were your parents during all of this?

They didn't know where I lived. They had no clue. I was so fucked up I just completely cut myself off from them.

Aside from the spent money, all this seems so free of repercussion.

Yeah [chuckles], luckily. I mean, for me it was; not for everyone. I didn't even know that repercussions were landing on people. One of my boys was driving a high-end Turbo in South Beach *in broad daylight* when he got lit up by four dudes with AK-47s. The thing is, there is so much poverty down there you can pay people to do anything. They say there is more crime in New York, but I never saw so much shit as when I was in Florida.

How many of your crew are still doing this?

Well, a lot of them are in hiding because of the DEA, the FBI. One is working on an oil rig. One is doing roofing in Arkansas. Another one is in South Carolina doing fishing charters. They just don't use credit cards; only cash. So they're in hiding. These kids stayed in the life, and they were in Florida where it was so hot I left the state.

You didn't worry about any of that heat from Florida coming back to you?

What I worried about is certain people finding my family. If anybody did search for me, my parents' address would be what would turn up. So I warned my family a lot. My dad had a gun, legally, in the house, just in case.

Did you ever tell your parents what you had been doing?

At the end of it I was sick and tired of everything so I came flat-out and told them. I was still in the LES, but I wasn't working. I was so fucked up on drugs. I needed to go to rehab, so I called my parents. [Pause.] Oxys are the one thing I'm a slave to.

How many days do you have?

[Chuckles.] Now, I mean, I have been back and forth with this shit. I've been clean for three weeks now.

Why do you think TV shows and movies about organized crime are so popular?

It's entertaining. A lot of people think about that life, but not too many people get to live it, to experience it.

Do you feel a sense of validation for having lived a life that is so celebrated by our society?

No, no. I'm not proud of what I did—by any means. There are people still in jail, there are people who are dead or are drinking through straws for the rest of their lives because of shit that we did to them. Why did we have to rob them? I should have gone out and gotten a job like everyone else.

Do you worry about an investigation catching up with you and your crew?

I still worry about that. You never know what they're going to find. The boss-kid got busted about a year ago. He posted bail by putting one of his houses up and ran. Like, these kids have *so much money.* They had houses, they had stash houses, they had grow houses. I mean, now he's got the DEA all over him. I'm not too concerned about what I did, just because I know there was no police activity when I was down there, and when I was up here there really wasn't any heat. If anything

I would be worried about somebody I robbed still holding a grudge. I mean, there are plenty of people who want my head right now. I ran into someone like that recently but thank god I was with like ten people and he was alone.

Do you ever see yourself going back to that kind of life?

There are times when I miss the money, but that's about it. If I ever did anything again I would just set up deals. I still know people, I know the suppliers. So I would just middleman it and take a cut.

Are you thinking about going back to college?

[Pause.] No.

ALEX

31, East Village

Do strangers ever ask you for drugs?

Yes, they do in fact. I don't think they ever think I'm the drug dealer, because if I was I wouldn't be on the street panhandling, but I think they assume—and, generally, they are correct—that I'm strung-out and in a tough situation, and that if they buy me something to get straight, I'll take care of them.

Who are these people who ask you to buy them heroin?

You would never pick them out on the street as being drug addicts. It makes me think of myself when I've been in new cities after I've been clean for years and then I fuck up…. You would never know I was a junky. These people totally look like clean-cut college kids, or some hipster types, or whatever. They'll come up and they'll be all sketched out and say, "Look, ah, I was just wondering if you, ah—*know where to get dope*?" [Chuckles.] I run them through a battery of questions and I feel them out.

What do you ask?

I've heard conflicting things about this, but apparently the one standard thing you ask is if the person is a cop or if they have anything to do with the cops. I heard that it can ruin a case against you if you are directly asking, "Are you a police officer or working for the police?" and they mislead you.* That being said, the cops could just lie in court since it's my word against theirs. Anyway, so I ask the person things and I watch their body language, their eye contact, and I determine whether to take a chance on them. A lot of it, too, has to do with how desperate I am. In the past there have been times when I was really sick and I took a chance even though I didn't have a good feeling about it. I've never had a problem; I've been lucky.

What's your finder's fee?

It depends on the person asking. I'm probably the least greedy, best person you'd hope to buy you your dope. If they're getting three $10-bags I'm only going to expect one. If we're staying in the Lower East Side, which is quick and convenient, a bundle is $90. (I know where to get a bundle for $50 or $60—which is a really good hook-up—but we'd have to go uptown.) But the rate is not a set-in-stone thing. I've also had people say they would split everything right down the middle with me, and I'll be like, "Oh, that's too nice, don't worry about it. Whatever."

So you leave your panhandling spot and go to your heroin dealer?

Sometimes I get the customer to just wait with my shit—a ratty-looking bag filled with blankets and things I need to survive—but usually they insist on coming with. I make it clear to them they can follow me but only from what I call a "running distance" where, if I suddenly bolt, they'd have a fighting chance to catch me. Another thing I always make clear is that I am dealing with someone who knows me and trusts me; if they were to roll up in the middle of the deal, it would make me look bad and it would probably kill the deal. Even if it doesn't, I will just give you your money back.

* According to *Police Field Operations* by Thomas F. Adams, this is a common misconception people have. Cops can lie; the case stands.

Do you ever catch any attitude?

People can be a bit grouchy because we're dealing with their money and even if they're not sick they've gotten themselves so worked up with anticipation. You know, these people coming up to me for dope aren't doing dope for the first time. They probably haven't done it for a while, and they may have struggled with addiction, so when they get it again their hands are shaking— they just can't wait to get it inside them.

You just divvy it up on the spot?

Well, when I get the dope from my guy I take out my cut right away so there isn't any chance of the customer trying to negotiate our deal after the fact. If there is some problem, the customer knows where to find me, and we go our separate ways. I try to be as quick about this as possible because this is a business-thing—I want to get back to my [panhandling] spot so I can keep making money, or so someone else can come up to me for dope. A lot of times, also, the customers are rarely outfitted with rigs and all the gear they need, so I usually provide that as well.

They'll take needles from you, a perfect stranger?

Well, it comes in a sealed package. Also, I'm pretty good at making small talk as I walk there and I'm pretty good at putting people at ease. I think people can tell pretty quickly that I'm not a scumbag. Honestly, I've never ripped anybody off out here; I have a really gold name. There are some other people who have some not-so-great names, but I'm known as a man of his word. When I was still using, I had a lot of customers who supported my habit. After a couple times dealing with me, people would get comfortable enough that I'd tell them to just meet me at the park, I'd be there.

Which park was your preferred meet up spot?

The spot over the summer was the East River Park, by the entrance on 6th Street. There's a bathroom right there where everybody shoots up because it's right where everybody picks up in the projects and you just have to go across the bridge. Sometimes people race across because they're all anxious and they dive into the men's room and [chuckles] get their shot as quick as possible. But it's also a very dangerous spot because cops come through there and they bust people all the time. Myself, I've gotten busted there twice.

In a Word on the Street New York interview you once mentioned getting busted while helping some people with their shots.

Yeah, I was helping them with their shot because they didn't know how to do anything, really.

Was it their first time shooting up?

No, what it was is they were used to dope but they also had coke, and they weren't used to shooting coke. With dope, if someone overdoses you can just hit them with Narcan and they'll snap out of it, but if someone OD's on coke, call a fuckin' ambulance; I don't know what to do because they could be having a heart attack. So what I did was measure out how much coke they were going to have in the first shot—if they want to do more in the next shot, that's fine—but I just don't want to see anything happen. It was also the day before the dude's wedding—

—Oh Christ.

I was not going to have it on my conscience that he went through me and, you know, he OD'd and died in some shithole bathroom on the day before his wedding. I'm just not going to do that to his bride. I'm just a softy, but he was so thirsty he was like, "Balls to the wall! Yeah!" He probably would have done the whole thing. I wanted him to be safe at what was pretty much his bachelor party.

What was this guy's story?

He lived in Brooklyn. I don't know what work he's doing now; he was kind of floundering around. I don't want to say too much about him because that's his business. So we're there in the bathroom and I have syringes for three different people in this stall and all of a sudden there is a head peeking over the door and it's a park employee. He was like, "If that toilet flushes, if you try doing anything…" He was ready to scoop me up. He had a partner right there who kicked the door in and grabbed everything and probably threw them out—I have no idea. He took my pack and when I said, "Hey, that's everything I own," he said, "Well, you should have thought about that before you came here." For all I know, the parks employee was just shysty and hoped there was something of value in my bag. At the time I was torn between wanting to argue to try to get my stuff and feeling like I should be happy he's not getting the police involved and I'm not going to jail. I regretted it because it was starting to get cold. [Pause.] You don't have a cigarette, do you?

No, I quit. What I did was I dipped pouch tobacco for a month—always swallowing it. I literally sickened myself of nicotine and tobacco.

That was your game plan?

Yeah, and it worked. It's been four years now, no problem.

[A smiling, elderly woman bends down and places a dollar in Alex's cup. He thanks her.]

A few months ago you stopped using heroin and got on a methadone program—I'm really proud of you. Do people still ask you to score them dope?

Yeah, still all the time. I'd say weekly. It's petered out—if you don't mind my using your name as a verb.

I don't.

So when people approach me it always starts out with some small talk: people ask me how I'm doing and I tell them I'm good, that I've started on a methadone program, I'm working on getting housing, and they get the hint. Sometimes they'll still ask if I know where to get anything, and I'll tell them, "Honestly, dude, not really. One dude I know just walked by but I don't even know his number. I can't really help you with that anymore."

Would it be tough for you to handle the transaction?

I have no interest. Honestly, that has been a really cool thing about being on methadone: I could have a brick, I could have a sleeve—five bricks—of dope and it'd be useless to me. Toward the end there—and I don't know how much I expressed this to you—I fucking hated doing dope, but it just became how I got by, how I survived. Of course I would get really sick if I didn't use, but also just psychologically being out here I had to stay a little fucked up. It sucks, it's miserable. I mean, you eat shit all day, people treat you like hell, and you just have to disassociate yourself a little bit. With opiates, you're happy and floaty no matter what—people can't really get you down. You're kind of untouchable. But the dope started sucking more and more anyway—and my tolerance was getting so high—that it just didn't make sense anymore. It was just stupid. Now, I take a dose once a day, and the longer I go there they'll give me take-home bottles.

Does methadone taste good?

It tastes fucking awful. It tastes like any medicine, like if you were to take aspirin and dilute it and mix it with cherry cough syrup.

If I were to take one of your daily doses right now, what would it do to me?

It would wreck you. You have to understand, too, that it lasts for 24 hours. Me, I have a really high tolerance so I'm taking a really high dosage right now. But if you were to take even 20 or 30 milligrams—something they would start you on if you had almost no habit—you would probably be slumped over like a dope head on the nod. If you drank my entire dose you'd probably die.

How many milligrams are you on?

180—it's pretty high.

What's the highest you've heard someone getting?

I've heard of people getting 240, but I don't personally know anyone who takes more than I do. But I feel OK. Do I seem OK?

You seem totally sober to me.

It's great. I don't feel high; I just don't feel sick.

What's the next phase of your life?

It's funny because I can see far ahead what I want, but regarding the next immediate thing I actually have to reflect on a conversation I had at this shelter I've been staying at, and there's this woman who's been staying there on parole. She is very obviously transgendered—I mean, she [assumes a gruff voice] "Talks like this, sweetie!"

You sound exactly like Alice in *Superjail!*

She's really caring. We had this long talk and she told me, "Honey, all you need to worry about is learning to love yourself." She pointed out things like how my nails are all messed up and that it's a simple thing to cut them and clean them. She said I had to take better care of myself, but that I had to start with baby steps. I hadn't thought of myself beyond the context of surviving the day for so long, and I had no hope for myself to have the things that anybody wants, like companionship or doing something with my time that makes me happy and maybe makes a difference—the things we're supposed to do as people. I need to get back into being in the world, and I'm tryin'. How that's going to go for me, I don't know, but I hope I can do it.

JOCEYLN

38, Gramercy Park

Have you ever been caught?

I have been caught. The one time I actually went out with anything on me to sell, I got caught.

It was the first time ever?

The first and only time.

[Laughs.] That's like a teenager having sex for the first time and getting pregnant.

Absolutely, 100%.

You're shaking your head and smiling now.

With respect to the analogy you just made, this was like

getting a girl pregnant on the first time because the condom broke. Under no circumstances should I have gotten caught; I didn't do anything to expose myself.

OK, let's get a bit of context: you are a lawyer. You and a partner were in a New Jersey parking lot in front of a Phish show selling weed and edibles.

[Laughs.] Oh god! See, that's the thing, we weren't working together.

You were concertgoers.

Correct. We go to a lot of Phish shows and he hustles weed at some of them. This one and only time, I brought rice crispy treats [edibles] to sell.

[Laughs.] This is great.

I know there are a lot of stereotypes here. Throughout 20 years I've seen well over 100 shows; all it takes is one time to fuck it up.

Phish concert parking lots are notorious drug bazaars.

They are. People sell clothes, tons of food, drugs—whatever you could possibly need you can find on the lot.

The Phish community seems very cohesive.

It is, but there are some dirtbags.

After 100 shows you must have a whole dresser drawer filled with tie-dyed Phish shirts.

[Laughs.] I don't own anything tie-dyed. What's really funny is that when I got clipped I was wearing a corduroy, floral-print dress that I made in high school that I hadn't worn since college. I took it back out, 'cause I lost some weight and it fit again, I was like, "I'm going to wear it [to the Phish show] just for the fuck of it." It made me look like a super hippie. In hindsight, that dress could have been something that contributed to my getting arrested.

OK, so you're there with your friend—

We have been going to shows together for years and we would make butter out of weed shake, because he used to grow. We'd smoke bowls and make boatloads of butter.

Sounds like fun.

Yeah, it is. You sit around, play a little Scrabble, and you send people home with butter. They sold it off, in sticks to people, because it's very versatile. People put it on toast, people put it on pasta—it's definitely a cleaner way to go. This time, a big part of the reason was the fact that I was super low on cash because New York sucks and it's really expensive. I decided that I would jump in on this, because we had all this butter, and we were making stuff anyway, so we made a shitload of rice crispy treats, probably 60. I didn't even have them all with me when I got clipped.

So you guys arrive at the lot...

It was a boardwalk. The idea is once you're in the lot, there's an insular feeling to it, but it's definitely peppered with cops. If you are seasoned, you kind of know what to expect, although sometimes you don't when you're going to a venue Phish has never played before. We had walked down from a nearby hotel.

So this was a big weekend for you guys?

Oh my god, yeah, it was Halloween weekend; Phish always does an amazing show. They play three sets and the middle set is a whole cover album of someone else. Halloween and New Year's Eve are the most coveted Phish tickets of the year. That's what we went down for—those three shows.

And you're really high the whole time because you're eating rice crispy treats.

No! The complete bitch of this was at the time I wasn't eating any carbs: no sugar, no rice, no nothing—so I didn't even get to eat these strong, crazy, rice crispy treats that everyone got knocked on the ass by and loved! The day of the first show, my friend and I take a walk down the boardwalk. I had a few with me in a big bag, 'cause I knew there would be people around. I wrapped them all individually in saran wrap, which in hindsight definitely opens you up for intention to sell. But after 20 years of going to shows, I knew who the tourists were and who were my people.

How so?

Just the way they were looking, talking, and acting. What's funny, to someone outside the community, there might be some blurry lines. You got people going who are frat kids with popped collars, but they might all be talking like they know what's going on; they're not just getting drunk and running around the casinos. Then you have your dreadlocked stereotype, walking around with hula-hoops and flowers and whatnot. And then there's anyone in between.

How do you distinguish a plainclothes cop?

Not very well apparently [laughs], because that's how we ended up in jail! If it's someone who is older and wearing white sneakers, you should have a heightened sense of caution.

OK, so this is when you guys get arrested. You're walking on the boardwalk with your rice crispy treats, your friend is selling weed...

It was a nice day, and I actually sold a couple on the boardwalk, just being like, "Heady rice crispy treats." It's like moths to a flame and I charged $5. As we got close to the venue there were people on top of people. I saw some guy ask my friend something. I knew what was transpiring, so I walked away. In my mind I was like, "Why did you start selling to the old guy?" I would say he was in his late 40s, and he was wearing those white sneakers that scream *cop*. So I broke off, not necessarily like, "Fuck you, you're on your own." We came to the show together, we made the rice crispy treats together, but he was selling weed—his deal—and I was selling rice crispy treats. I heard a commotion and just moved away. I looked over and he looked at me, and the cops looked at me, and I was just standing there like, "What the fuck?" My first instinct was to take my bag of rice crispy treats and throw them in the trash can, but before I could do that, I heard, "Drop your bag and put your hands behind your back."

I'm like, "What's going on?" Three cops swarmed me and the next thing I knew I was in those plastic, zip-tie cuffs they always tie way too tight. I was standing there and I couldn't even process what was going on. Some fucking kid came up and was like, "Yo, can I buy your ticket?" I was like, "Are you fucking kidding?" One of the cops told me I should sell it to him because I wasn't going anywhere soon, but the other cop said I'd be out in an hour. I hedged in favor of going to the show. It was fucked up; the cops perp-walked us through the crowd. I was that girl.

Which is kind of funny.

In hindsight it's really funny.

How did the cops know your rice crispy treats were criminal?

That's a really good question—they didn't. They had no probable cause to come near me. Not only did they not catch me doing anything, they didn't even know what was in the bag. So they perp-walked us to this holding area underneath the venue and there were a couple people in zip ties. They didn't question me at first at all, and they didn't Mirandize me. They had tables spread out so they could empty bags, and we were standing there waiting. My friend was like, "Don't say anything; if they ask, tell them what was in your bag was all mine and you didn't know what was in it."

Wow, that's really nice.

It was really nice. However, possession is nine-tenths of the law; even though they didn't know what was in the rice crispy treats, they'd gotten me. My friend said something about me being a lawyer, and some cops overheard and said, "Oh, you're gonna get disbarred! Haha!"

Were you scared by that notion?

For almost two years I was shitting a brick. Eventually my friend asked if I had anything else on me and I told him I had a little personal stash and a one-hitter. He told me I might as well just tell them. There was this one lady cop I told and she was so nice.

She didn't laugh at you as well?

No, she was actually concerned [about the possible disbarment]. She said she hoped things worked out. She moved me out of view, patted me down, and took the one-hitter—I don't know what happened to my little personal stash—I could have been easily charged with paraphernalia, but I wasn't. She was the only nice person I dealt with the whole time. Later, we got put in a paddy wagon, and it's split down the middle, and I'm the only girl. It's six dudes on the other side of this metal fence thing, I'm in the back and I'm sitting right across from my friend. He's like, "Don't panic, don't panic." I have tremendous medicated anxiety, but I kept my composure the whole time, which is kind of uncharacteristic.

Had you been charged at this point?

No, they didn't know for months! They said to me, "Oh, what's that?" I was like, "Rice crispy treats." "What's in them?" "Rice and marshmallows." "Oh, what else?" "Butter." That was it, I never said anything to incriminate myself; I'm not fucking retarded. We got to the police station and I went with the girls and he went with the guys. Now I'm by myself, face-palming for a few hours when they put this little 18-year-old girl from Arkansas in my cell. I'm pretty sure she was selling acid because she was out of her mind. The cops were just being completely disgusting, disrespectful douchebags, like they were on *Jersey Shore*. They were yelling, "OK, who's DTF?" That's "down-to-fuck."

Oh Christ.

Yeah, so the cops are yelling this, and this fucking bitch in my cell is like, "Oh, me!" I'm like, "Shut the fuck up!" That's the only time I lost my composure. I'm like, "You're in here with me, I'm absolutely not DTF, and if you think about it, neither are you."

The cops must have been excited by her announcement.

She was being an asshole and said, "Whatever it takes to get out of here." The cops come back down, gave her shit, and walked away.

Did they flirt with her?

Yeah, but they also acknowledged she was nuts. She was yelling and screaming that she made a deal and she should be out by now. Three or four cops look back at her and tell her she has coke all over her face.

Jesus.

My friend [was moved past my cell] to get his mug-shot taken and to get fingerprinted and he told me I was going to be all right. I learned after the fact that the cops told him that I was ratting him out. He's like, "No she didn't and no she's not." A few minutes later, I get walked back there and get the same deal, picture, and fingerprints, and the cops tell me that he ratted me out, and they again tell me I'm going to get disbarred.

Yikes.

The cops let my friend and me out together, pretty much onto the boardwalk, and the Phish show had just let out. Everyone was walking around talking about how it was the greatest show ever.

That's an added twist of the knife.

Yeah. Walking down the boardwalk, I was absolutely incredulous: there are fucking nitrous tanks as far as the eye can see. That's an innate part of the lot-scene—the telltale sound of a nitrous tank [makes an air-tank sound]. Here, down the boardwalk, it was just people surrounded by tank, tank, tank. My friend bought a couple of balloons, and I was like, "Are you fucking kidding me?" He was like, "What the fuck else are we gonna do?"

Were you extra sketched out about plainclothes cops?

At that point, I didn't even know how to process. I was just walking in a complete fucking daze—I'd never been arrested. I'm thinking, I'm so pissed because nitrous is much more egregious, obvious, and dangerous than anything going on here. Within the whole Phish community you hear about the "Nitrous Mafia" at every show. Is someone running protection for them? Eventually we made it back to our hotel and I called a few friends to see if anyone knew attorneys in Jersey. We got a hold of a guy who worked with a family-friend of a friend of mine, he and his partner both did NY and NJ, so he came down [for my court appearance that Monday].

You guys went back to your hotel?

Mhm. We smoked a couple of bowls, made the best of it. The next day we woke up and were like, "What the fuck?" I still had ten treats left; you know I wasn't going to do anything with them.

When did the charges come? Those rice crispy treats went to a lab, right?

Yeah, and the charges didn't come back for months. Was I going to get disbarred? I figured there wasn't any possibility of me going to jail, because the cops never had probable cause—they had no grounds to search me. That didn't mean I wasn't fucking scared shitless, because I was.

So often cops treat a person being scared as reason enough to detain them, interrogate them, and arrest them—which is plenty reason for a person to be scared of cops. What kind of law do you practice?

My substantive experience is legal unemployment and civil rights. The irony of it right? I spend all this time trying to help people. [Pause.] A whole bunch of time goes by and there's no discovery, no anything. They indicted us without ever even telling us, because I guess in New Jersey they can do that. We get this paperwork with all the indictments, and I just blew a gasket in my lawyer's office, "What the fuck is this?! What about a grand jury?" He's like, "In New Jersey, they can convene without you." I get the paperwork and it's such bullshit. They contradicted themselves within the packet of discovery. You should take a look at it if you're into reading fiction. Here were the charges: possession of more than five grams of hash but less than a pound of hash—although I didn't have any hash on me; 4th degree, manufacture, distribution, dispense, more than one ounce of weed, but less than five pounds. This was all taken out of the food product once they eventually got around to it.

Oh, OK.

Which, by the way, was in April and this happened in October. I had three felonies: a 4th degree, two 3rd degrees, and a 2nd degree. [I was charged with possessing] more than an ounce, but less than five pounds of weed; more than five grams, but less than a pound of hash; then a conspiracy charge with that same breakdown; and then possession/distribution within 500 feet of a public housing facility—second degree.

Yikes.

There was stuff in there that was complete lies and complete distortions. My lawyer saw me turn redder and redder 'cause I was angry as fuck, because it was all bullshit; all I wanted to do was to fight this. It would have been in his interest to go to trial, 'cause that's a lot more fees on his part, even if I don't win. But he said he didn't want me to go to trial because I wasn't in a mental state where I would have been able to deal—not because I was crazy or anything, but because of my anxiety—and he was right. He said we were going to do the conditions of this pretrial intervention thing so I'd have a chance to get it completely expunged, like it never even happened. If we had gone to trial it would have become a huge, fucking expensive debacle—which would have been public record, by the way. I guess I was an upstanding enough member of society that [the courts] gave me a chance [with the pretrial intervention]. There was a whole bunch of conditions: 40 hours of community service; a $50 enrollment fee into the PTI program; $35 "safe neighborhood assessment" fee; $2,000 in fines; $150 in lab charges—so they can sit on my stuff for six months and come back with bullshit levels; and a $50 D.A.R.E. fee.

A cop who taught D.A.R.E. at my high school later got caught selling weed.

I also had to test for substance abuse, forfeit the money that they seized from my wallet—$198 which they jacked. Like I said, fuck New Jersey, but I was like, let's just fucking do this thing because I wanted to be done with this two-year program of having to go to fucking rehab, three days a week, for rice crispy treats.

Where you go to a clinic and they talk about believing in god and being sober?

No, no, there's no god talk, 'cause I would not have done that. This was one that was reputable, and very accommodating of my situation. I had to do three days a week. I had to piss in a cup and talk for a fucking hour.

About weed?

Well, it was a very interesting place because the evening groups were the more professional people who were there because they got a DWI and were mandated by the court. Or they were there because they had a coke problem or whatever. They weren't necessarily in trouble, but they thought it would be a good idea to go to rehab. The people during the day were a whole other kind of demographic: your heroin people, your crack people. It was really interesting to see that kind of dichotomy.

This whole time you knew if you jumped through all these hoops, all the charges would be expunged?

Nothing was guaranteed, but yeah, that was the deal.

So after you finished the rehab program...

I finished it and I filed for dismissal, and I got dismissed. Then I was told, only at that point, that I could first file for expungement six months from then. I thought this was fucking done. No. I had to serve eight or nine different offices in New Jersey with certified mail. It was like over $10 per piece. I had to serve an order of dismissal. Then I had to file an order of expungement, that's another service, another couple hundred dollars once I add it all up. I got my expungement order eventually, with which they took their sweet-ass time, and it was almost two years to the day. And then I had to serve that, it was like hundreds on top of all the rest of this shit. I probably spent $6,000 altogether.

On top of what you paid your lawyer, which was how much?

Oh my god yeah, I got really lucky with him. I paid him a $1,500 retainer, and then I paid him another $1,500. If I was some random shmuck off the street, he wouldn't even deal with me for under $10,000, so I was very lucky. He understood what it was like to have law school loans—I was and am still paying $1,000 a month. But when I look back now, it could have been so much worse, but at the time it felt like the worst thing in the world. One tiny false move and I was going to be fucked for life. It was terrifying. I never told my mom; she still doesn't know. My sister does because she had to lend me the retainer.

How do you feel about all this chaos and stress, given the fact that weed will probably be legalized in most American states in like 10 years?

I think that it's criminal—and I don't use that word lightly—the resources that are spent on fighting an unwinnable war steeped in nothing but a very strong alcohol and tobacco lobby. I'm not practicing right now, but it's definitely in my mind that I would love to be able to help people out, especially in my community, where people get targeted and clipped left and right. I would like to be able to be a resource for people who were in my position. I have a friend who is also an attorney, also a huge Phish head, and we would love to be able to do a practice for people in that situation. We're at all the shows anyway.

It sounds like you'd have a thriving client base.

It's a niche market.

You'd be thinking like the cops: shooting Phish in a barrel.

[Laughs.] Touché. It really is. Once you rope them into the parking lot, it really is.

Has your enthusiasm for Phish music and culture waned since this incident?

The opposite; I've never been more into it. I took this whole experience and separated it from going to shows and enjoying the music. In the last couple years I've gone to 20 Phish shows, and—I expect people to laugh at me when I say this—I've found it to be my happy place. That's where I'm the most at peace. Like I said, the feeling of the music and the community is really indescribable. A Phish show is supposed to be a fun, happy place. For me, it still is, and now it is even more so.

WALTER

30, East Village

What do you think of your former customers?

Not very highly. [Laughs.]

No?

Generally no.

Why not?

I dealt with a lot of customers who were not the best people.

Why not?

Because I'd walk into a $3,000,0000 apartment and there would be empty pizza boxes and takeout everywhere. The apartment would be trashed, and they'd be bitching about the economy. These are annoying people, generally, in Manhattan.

Did you have any customer pet peeves?

When customers grab my weed case and just start digging through it. That annoyed me because I'm pretty organized and would have different kinds and different volumes. Overall what annoyed me is people not being there when they said they would be, not answering their phone when I showed up on point: the usual messenger shit. Granted, [a weed courier] is just a service provider, but you're also juggling 13 other runs, and time. That can get hectic.

Have you had any residual grudges from having to scold a customer?

I guess sometimes you'll get an address and you're like, "Fuck, it's that dude." I'm not one to hold grudges; at the end of the day it's just a customer. Why should I stress my day out because they're idiots who don't know how to purchase drugs?

We're just talking weed?

Yeah, I never wanted to get involved otherwise. Late hours, weird customers—it's high risk.

Did your company ever consider offering other substances?

People would ask all the time, and there are services out there that do, but I chose not to work for any of them. I mean, I'm racing and doing a bunch of other bike stuff—it was just a job to me. My life is more important than some custies and what they want.

That's drug dealer slang you just employed, *custies*?

Yeah.

Sounds like boogers.

They're probably equivalent, you know.

Yeah, it wasn't all bad. Twenty percent of people were annoying as shit, but it's like that with any service industry job. There are like-minded people that either have done the job or have been around weed so long that they know the game. Most weed heads are creative on some level, I figure. You're delivering for a guy for two years, and you see him working on paintings—eventually there's going to be some conversation. You see cameras in a girl's spot, and you're a photographer, eventually you're gonna bring up photography. So if you can relate on some level, it makes the job more enjoyable.

Did you become friends with any of the customers?

A couple. I'm also very leery of people, but when people are genuine, I can see it. Like I said, when you deliver to someone for two years, you can gauge whether someone is a good person or not.

Were you ever called somewhere and you arrived at the same time as another dealer selling something else?

Yeah.

How has that gone?

It's only happened a couple of times. Both times the other guy was trying to bro down about the job, and I didn't really care or want anything to do with it.

He was selling the same thing as you?

Yeah, and some other stuff too, he was like, "Oh, how's your day, busy?" I was like, "I don't want to talk about it."

You're like a FedEx guy and a UPS guy in a freight elevator.

[Laughs.] I think so. They'll talk about the weather—whatever small talk—to make the situation less weird.

Did he ride a bicycle?

I assume so.

How long have you known about this unique-to-New York bike trade?

Probably about 12 years. But New York is not the only place that has it; almost every major city has some sort of form of it.

You think so?

I know there is in San Francisco and LA. In Portland there is, but it's not a straight-up serve, it's some guy who sells weed on a bike and cruises around. I used to have my own serve in Seattle.

What was your hiring criteria?

I worked for myself, and I had close friends who needed extra work, so I put them on.

So it's a matter of a person already being your trusted friend?

Sure, at the end of the day it's my product and my money.

Did you ever hire someone who was a referral from a friend?

Never.

Why not?

I didn't trust very many people.

Why not?

It was my product and my money.

You were afraid people would be robbed? Or rob you?

Not robbed. It's that I don't know their personality inside and out, so I can't gauge how they perceive themselves or how they carry themselves when I can't see them. If they get robbed, it still comes out of my pocket. What if they fuck up, get hit by a car, or get arrested, you know?

It's nice that you would have eaten the loss. I've heard of some serves when it falls on the runner.

It never came to that. Seattle is very neutral, mellow, liberal, and West Coast. It's very chill. Also it was a side gig; it wasn't an official serve that starts at noon and ends at midnight. I started at 6 p.m. and ended at 1 or 2 a.m., depending on the after work crowd. They seemed to pay better, and people bought in larger quantities, so it was less work on my end and we could still turn a high profit.

You worked a straight messenger job, then you would go home and put weed in your backpack?

And I would race on the weekends. I had to support my racing. That's why I needed a couple of friends to help out; I was getting burned out. I was also 20 years old. You're a little more durable in your youth.

It's funny, I can't help but make a comparison, or to think of racing as this addiction you're trying to finance. That's a lot of time on a bike—selling weed and racing on the weekend.

Messengering doesn't pay shit, that's the reality of it. Other messengering pays twice as much. Racing is expensive, man. If you're not sponsored, a $3,000 carbon road frame is out of your reach unless you have other ways to get it. And without a frame like that, it's hard to perform well. Equipment, travelling—it adds up quick. After you're set and have your equipment, then it's just maintenance. I needed to come up with a way to get an initial investment to go to the next level of racing, and selling weed was how I could do it.

What was your experience with the New York serve?

We were four on bikes, set up in zones, and we would rotate zones two or three times a day so plainclothes cops wouldn't see us. The zones were 125th to 57th streets, 57th to 23rd, 23rd to probably Grand Street, or maybe Delancey, and Delancey and down. There was a guy in a car that would just do picks and drops. You'd run out, meet him, and get more weed.

That's very interesting, the way you shifted zones throughout the day.

Yeah, you don't want to be in the same zone all day, you know. You could tell [the dispatcher], "I saw a couple of plainclothes cops, rotate me." You got to keep an eye out if you see people looking at you. Generally you're probably fine, but none of us want to get fucked with, so we just rotated.

Beyond keeping an eye out for plainclothes, what else would you do?

Not wear a messenger bag or a backpack; wear some computer laptop bag, just to blend in with the Lincoln Square crowd. If you know you're going to work Uptown most of the day, look like you live on the Upper West Side. If you're working Downtown, you just wear whatever, but dress clean and presentable.

How would you dress when you worked on the Upper West Side?

Khakis with a button down shirt, with some pomade in your hair, you know. [Laughs.] Some boat shoes, I used to wear wallabies because they were comfortable. I'd just try to blend in and play the game.

How did you arrive at the decision to change up your appearance?

After about a year or so of doing it, you start to see the same fucking cops, in the same areas, around the same times. I'm hyper observant, so I figured it was the safe route. I don't want to get caught—I got too much shit on the line.

What do you have on the line?

Racing, girlfriend, people that rely on me.

Did your girlfriend care you worked for a weed service?

No, the girl I'm dating now wouldn't care, she would probably want me to get her pieces so she could smoke. The girl I was dating at the time said she didn't, but I'm pretty sure she did. We would get into fights about it and all this shit. You know, it's hard to turn down a decent amount of cash. I think what it really came down to is she was bummed that she was busting her ass in an office and I was making essentially twice as much as her.

Well, your job is dangerous and it's very labor intensive.

Yeah, I'd come home tired. It's a physical job.

Did she have any issue with the illegality of your job?

I was writing a ton of graffiti previously, and she went through all that. I'd always been on the opposite side of the law. That's how she knew me, I don't think it was too much of a surprise. I don't think she necessarily liked it, but it was one of those things she had to accept.

Do you still write?

Nope, same reason I don't sell weed. I'll go paint a tunnel or abandoned freight, some abandoned building, sure, but I'm not out trying to street bomb.

Do you miss the weed courier work?

No. I was a traditional messenger for ten years previous. I've worked on my bike since I was eight years old. I'm 30 now. Sure, the romance is still there, but I did it. I raced, I traveled, I messengered multiple cities, had a good time; it's good to end on a high note. I'm not trying to make it my career.

Do you know people who seem intent on making it a long-term thing?

Sure, it's like bartending, or any other service job where you make a lot of money, cash in hand. Sometimes it's hard to turn down. Some people don't know what to do, they've been doing something so long. I have friends over 40 who are bartenders, and they started when they were in their 20s.

Do you feel like their job distracted them from things or projects that they wanted to do?

Sure, I think most people's do for that matter. The idea is you're living this alternative lifestyle to accommodate whatever creative outlet you are either funding or making time for. Oftentimes you are too tired to work on your creative stuff 'cause you worked in the snow for ten hours—it's a tough balance. I've seen people actually pull it off who are doing quite well for themselves now, and left selling weed to pursue their art, or pursue whatever creative medium they are intrigued by. But, more often than not, you see kids kind of get stuck in the loop. Mainly from partying and drinking, 'cause you have a ton of cash in hand, and you go out to the bar after your workday and see your friends. I used to go straight home. If I wanted to drink I'd get a six-pack and invite a friend over or something. I was also saving up for a goal.

Would you ever revel in the glamour of the job?

Glamour?

The excitement of doing something illegal and lucrative?

No, it was just a job for me. I grew up with my parents growing weed—I sold weed from 15–16 on—to me it was just a job. What I did like about it, and the same thing about traditional messaging, is that I was always out with a camera and I got some of my best shots, in my opinion, being out there on a bike. I miss that aspect, a lot, but that's the only thing I miss. I didn't really revel in the lifestyle too much, it was just customers and a product. It could have been selling apples or oranges. I don't smoke weed anymore, so to me it's not a thing.

Did your parents know you were doing this while you were doing it?

I moved out when I was 14; it wasn't really up to them what I was doing.

I'm sure it wasn't up to them, but did you tell them?

Sure.

And they weren't mad?

I'm sure my mother would like to see me do something else, but I also think she sees why I was doing it. You work with the cards you are dealt, and I had to make my own deck. I mean, she's glad I don't do it anymore, mainly for legal reasons and safety, but she knows I'm smart in that regard.

Have any of your messenger friends been stopped by the NYPD?

I have a friend who got bagged 'cause the cops had seen this guy around, walking his bike, so they shook him down and got some stuff. They were in the back of a cop car, going down a street, and the cops saw two more guys on bikes and were like, "Oh, we are going to get those guys next, we see them all over. All you guys look the same—you got to switch it up." [Later] they interrogated him for three or four hours, good cop/bad cop routine.

How did that go?

He was just like, "You're not going to get anything out of me. Just give me the charge," essentially. They did. It was his second time getting arrested, so he had a bunch of fines to pay and community service. Whether he's done all that, I'm not sure.

So the tip from those cops: Don't look like a bike messenger.

Right.

So many weed couriers won't stop dressing the part, though. Whether they're in traffic, waiting on a light, or at a bar, they want people to know they're legit. They just don't want to shed the cloak of their tribe.

[Laughs.] *The cloak of the tribe* is a good way to put it. It's almost like a comic book character they make up in their head—they perceive themselves as some superhero. I mean, it's a job right? Sometimes you got to wear a uniform for a job. For [selling weed] I blended in and I never got asked once what I was doing in a building. If you dress like a bike messenger, at 11 p.m. on the Upper West Side, you're gonna get stopped. I've seen plenty of kids get caught because they won't shed that cloak. To me it's a foolish pride-thing: "I'm a bike messenger." Oh, you can't stop pedaling and you deliver weed all day? Congratulations. [Laughs.]

ANGUS

Age Not Disclosed, Bed-Stuy

How did you get started with this marijuana delivery service?

It started the day I got back on my bicycle, back in fucking January 2011. Oh, wait. [Holds out an inch-long hair for me to see.] Can you believe I pulled this out of my nose?

That's disgusting. Just now?

No, a long time ago.

I see you keep it with you.

This thing grew from the top of my *nose*. It's pretty crazy, right? It was only sticking out a little bit from the bottom, like it must have been—

—Dude, please put that away. That's so gross.

Alright, I'll put it back in my little drug box.

Great. Continuing.

I had just recovered from a fractured ankle and I went on craigslist for half an hour and found a fucking food delivery job in the city. I worked that stupid-ass shit for a single day. I'm about to roll out when I see one of my old friends from a courier company I worked at. Two years ago this guy got in a serious bike accident and broke his collar bone and shit. I carried his bike and bag from 57th and Lexington all the way down to the office, over a mile. I never felt he owed me a favor or anything, but when I run into him now he asks me if I need a job. I'm like, "Yeah dude, get me anything better than this place." He said, "Just call this number in the morning and see if they give you any work. I owe you for carrying my bike down." I was like, "Cool."

Aww.

I went the next day and rode down to South Brooklyn—way fucking deep—and met up with the dispatcher. I locked my bike up by the subway station he told me to meet him at and he pulled up in a car and told me to get in. There were mad cell phones ringing, but he wouldn't answer any of them. He asked me a couple quick questions while we drove around. He goes, "Here's the deal…" and gives me a bag of fucking weed. "So, this is your fucking shit, you have your number." He dropped me back off at my bike. I started the next day.

This bag of weed was how big?

There were probably 50 bubbles in there.

A bubble was how many grams?

2.5.

Wait, what's a bubble?

You know when you put 25¢ in the candy machine and one of

those things pops out? It was one of those. It was pretty chill man. Almost everyone who worked at this service was either walking or longboarding, so me and this other guy on a bike owned this service. I busted my ass and I made money. I would nudge the dispatcher for more runs. After about two or three weeks of that, they asked me if I knew anybody else that was as fast as me. So I put my friend Hollywood J on. We worked that service to the ground.

What were the shift hours?

We took calls from noon to ten, but I would still take some after that.

You were only in Manhattan?

Yeah. The funniest thing to me is not only how lucrative it is, but how many people who run this fucking city call us. I'm delivering to the heads of corporations and shit, HBO and BET, like main motherfuckers. I'm going into the offices and dropping off serious weed for secretary after-parties. It's just funny to me how much money there is in something that is so illegal.

It shouldn't surprise you that something illegal is lucrative.

Yeah, it's just funny to me, man. I mean, I'm a good person but this is what I feel like I've been pushed to do. The best way I've been able to earn money here has been selling drugs— just weed mostly. But do you know what I mean? Society is pushing me to sell weed on my bike instead of working a real job. My mom raised me right, she put a good head on my shoulders, she taught me right and wrong and the power of hard work and determination. But this society that I'm living in has made me realize that it doesn't really work like that. I can work at the Food Dimensions and get $7.50 an hour, but for what? To be unhappy? This is the easiest thing; you make money really quickly if you have the balls to do it. It's about balls and wits. Some people wouldn't feel comfortable carrying drugs with them all the time, but I'll do it.

So how did you pick up?

Well, I'd meet a dude. It wouldn't be every day. It would be every other day, or every two days. I'd get a call in the morning, and I'd have my envelope with all the money and shit from the other night or past couple of days. He'd say, "Hey, come meet me I'm over here on this street and this street." I'd get $10 for each $50 I sold.

Really? That's double what most runners get paid.

You know, this service trusted its messengers too much to be honest, and that's why I think it went downhill.

So you get the 50 bubbles, in like what, a plastic bag?

No, they would vacuum-seal 50 bubbles in turkey bags. Once you open the vacuum seal, that shit's gonna just stink. I would squeeze everything in a turkey bag, squeeze all the air out and tie it in a knot. I have a Velcro-sealed secret compartment in the bottom of my messenger bag where I keep everything. That's gotten me out of a couple situations.

You've been stopped?

Yeah, and to this day I've never been arrested for selling weed. This one time in Bushwick I was riding my bike to these girls' apartment with a pound of weed hidden in my bag. I turn the wrong way onto their block 'cause it's like two blocks farther when I hear *whoop whoop!* There's a police van coming toward me. I'm like, "Oh shit, I got a warrant." The cops slow down and one sticks his arm out. "Stop! Didn't you hear me? Put your bike down, open your bag!" I'm like, "Chill out, what's going on, what's going on?" He's like, "I'm blowing my siren, you're going the wrong way, what are you doing, yo? What's in the bag?" I'm like, "Man, I got nothing in here."

Did the cop really say "Yo"?

No, that's just me talking. So by this time I've gotten off my bike and I dump everything in my bag on the ground. The cops ask if I've got any warrants. I'm like, "Actually officer, I do got a warrant." I tell him the warrant is only for riding a bicycle on the sidewalk and the cop says, "You know what, get out of here." They didn't take me in for some reason and they drive off. I was sitting there going like, "Holy shit, that was an act of god." So I get back on my bike and I meet these fucking girls on the roof of their building. We hang out for a while and I'm not even drinking a beer or nothing. It starts getting dark when the lights turn on and two fucking police officers come up from the stairs onto the roof! I'm like, "What the fuck is this?" The cops say we're not supposed to be on the roof and ask for IDs. None of these girls have their IDs on them, and the cops look at me like, "Pssh, we know *you* got an ID." I pull out my ID and say, "Man, I *just seen* you guys. I told you I have a warrant right now. [Other cops] let me go before for going the wrong way. Like, please, I'm having a horrible night, you just got to give me a break." They take my ID and say they have to search my bag. Yo, this woman cop who searched it must have either been retarded or on my side because she didn't see a little bag of weed in there among the clutter. She throws everything back in my bag, sits me down, like, "OK, you're cool, just chill out." I didn't know it but on the other side of this roof there is a whole bunch of other people watching a movie on a projector, and apparently a bunch are drinking underage so the cops are running IDs and checking for warrants. At this point the white shirt—the sergeant—walks up and says, "Yo, what the fuck is taking so long? Who's got warrants? Bring 'em in." The same cop from before comes over and says, "Sorry, man, but I'm going to have to see that ID again." I was like, "Oh, no, what do you mean?" "We gotta take you in." "No, man, you said I was cool, dude. Man, this sucks *so* hard." The guy let me grab some extra clothes to put on because if you go to central booking in the summertime in a wife-beater and shorts you'll be freezing...and when the cops weren't looking I was able to put a couple cigarettes under the sweatband of my hat. But the cops were cool because I feel like they gave me a little respect. They let me leave my bike, my phone, and even my bag—which still had that pound of weed hidden in it—at the girls' apartment.

You are wildly lucky.

The weirdest thing is when they were processing me [at the station house] this cop was being really cool. He takes down my birthdate and he's like, "Oh, I was born on the same day and year as you." It was so weird to hear that from someone who was arresting me. He said, "Man, I really was trying to give you a break, but that other dude fucked it up with that warrant shit." He asked me if I had anything illegal in my pockets—and I did have a one-hitter and a little bag of weed—so I gave it to him and he went and put it in his personal locker. When I got out of bookings the next day, I went back to the [station house] he met me outside and gave it back to me. It was a pretty crazy experience.

It's funny to think that on the day you were born there was another little baby in a hospital on the other side of the country who would arrest you 20-some-years later, and he would appreciate that fact.

Yeah, I know! [Chuckles.] I still have all these unanswered questions.

WOLF
35, Murray Hill

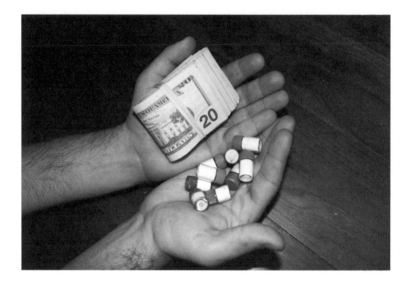

What's your side job?

Which side job are you talking about? [Laughs.] I'm a bartender, I'm a photographer, and on the occasion when it's convenient I'm somebody who provides for others.

You work with friends in "providing" for others?

Yes, I work under a friend; I probably wouldn't do it any other way. It's because it's a friend and I've known him for a while, and because it's a relatively stress-free relationship. Well, that's not always true. [Laughs.]

It seems like it couldn't be anything but stressful.

Sometimes, yeah, when things don't add up. I mean, maybe

before the issue is fully laid out it can be a little argumentative. Ultimately, I don't ever feel like it can't get resolved through discussion or just compromising. It's never like if I don't have all the money I should worry about my health or something.

So when the till is off, it doesn't necessarily come out of your pocket?

Sometimes it does, and sometimes it's waived—it depends on the circumstances. Sometimes I pay it back when I can.

That sucks, but it seems like it's just the way it is.

If you're short, you're short.

What's the most you've been short?

There was a time when I was like $500 short, because I had misplaced a few. I was worried that I was that careless, "How could I come up this short?"

I guess little vials of cocaine are easy to misplace.

Then I found them later. I happened to be moving, so in the move I had them in some sort of plastic bin and I forgot that I put them there.

Oh, that must have been a relief. Had you already paid him back that sum?

If it's ever one or two, it's never a big deal. But because it was five, he was upset. I don't remember what he said, but he definitely took it easier on me than he could have. As far as what I owed, he cut it in half, because he realized it was a mistake.

So how does it work, do you always have stuff on you?

I always keep it within reach. I'm a pretty low volume distributor, there's only a handful of people I deal with.

Those people tend to be friends of these people that you trust?

Yeah, they just tend to be clients for a while.

Do you have a certain jurisdiction?

What do you mean by that?

Is there a street you guys don't go above or below?

It's not really based on neighborhoods; it's just based on wherever it needs to go. It's not like we cut people off because it's in some other neighborhood that we don't go to.

So it's not just Manhattan or Brooklyn?

You travel if it's worth it. Sometimes they'll throw you some chip for a cab.

Do you use your personal phone, or do you have a burner phone?

I actually don't have a burner and that's probably really not a good idea. At the same time, I'm not high profile enough to worry about that. In some sense somebody might say I'm crazy, that I should always worry about it.

Sometimes text messages get pulled up in court.

That's why generally in text messages you try to be as unclear as possible.

How does a customer convey what they want?

Sometimes they mess up and I deliberately play stupid. Typically I have them ask for tickets. You know, "Do you have any tickets for the show? I need two." That's two $100 vials.

Hmm. What are your hours like?

One of the reasons why my friend has loyal clients is because he doesn't really limit his service to cut-off times. As for me, I don't go out really late at night or early in the morning anymore because I have other things going on that conflict. Also, if somebody says I want one, and they live in Battery Park City, I'm not going to go.

[Laughs.] I'd go to Battery Park City for three.

And then you would just hop on the train?

Yeah.

Do you ever bring a book?

I don't really read when I'm traveling. I just listen to music.

Are you keeping a look out?

I mean, I'm an unassuming person; no one's really looking at me.

Why not?

I don't seem like a coke dealer to a lot of people.

Do you put care into your outfits when you do this?

No.

You don't spiff it up a little extra?

No, not at all. If anything I dress down.

I heard of a coke dealer who always wears really nice suits and only sells to finance guys. He won't go above Chambers Street or something because he walks. Apparently he's been doing this for 15 years and has never been stopped.

If I sold coke to that extent I would probably dress up, too, but I don't even give it much thought. If I happen to be in a suit, it's incidental. I just go and generally meet these people in a secure place—not out in the open—do it real quick and keep moving. I'm not a prowler, one of these dudes trying to maximize his time out there. I'm trying to go and come back and continue with my life.

So how much on average do you make a month doing this?

I would say I could make more than I do if I took more of the opportunities, but sometimes I can't. Even with that consideration I still make $1,800, maybe?

Does that cover your rent?

Yeah, but I have other expenses that are pretty substantial, too. I look at it like this: selling coke enables me to not be obstructed by a full-time job, something that I ultimately don't really want to do. So basically I'm just trying to have time to put effort into the things I want to do.

Like taking photos?

And writing. I ultimately want to [go from working part-time to full-time] in the music industry. I also produce music. I'm working on an eight-to-ten track sampler album to show people my musical styles. It can be used for scoring television and movies or for a commercial spot. I wouldn't be able to do that, and devote as much time to it, without selling coke.

You're a starving artist who eats well.

Yeah, but I'm surviving without saving. The other thing is it allows me to live here, alone. I'm not a good roommate. So [privacy] and time are the luxuries that selling coke affords me. I don't think this is sustainable for years, by any means. But for now I have the time to go out and shoot at night when otherwise I'd be getting sleep to get up in the morning.

Between selling coke and bartending, you deal with lots of people in varying states of intoxication. Some of these people must be true addicts.

It's true that I encounter people in both trades, but I wouldn't say that I'm great at either of them. I'm certainly not a talkative bartender. I'm not one of those people that you can chop it up with about the neighborhood.

Do you do coke?

No.

Never?

I smoke weed *religiously* but I've only tried blow once. About a month ago I did a couple key bumps with some friends—that was the only reason I tried it.

Did you have trouble angling the key to your nostril?

No, I got it in all right. I guess a lot of people say you don't enjoy it the first time, but it didn't make me curious to try it again. I just felt very anxious, nervous, and high strung.

In selling coke have you ever had any scares or shitty experiences?

Never a scare but once it was shitty. I went all the way out to the depths of Queens, some ghetto suburb. I couldn't contact my guy at first and when he did show up he was $80 short and he had to go get more money. So he was an asshole. But as I said man, people I deal with are average people. They are everyday people who, when they go out on Friday and Saturday night, coke's their action. I don't really go to people I don't know, and I've never gone to a place I was worried to be at.

You're never worried about a cop waiting for you outside?

Because, like I said, I do really small volume. I don't really walk around with it, I take what I need, and that's it.

What's the highest level of education you have?

I have a master's degree in philosophy of education. [Laughs.] It's not like I have a certification or qualifications to go start teaching somewhere.

It seems like you could teach educational theory at a university.

I got the degree for good measure, but I did it more to live in Europe.

How wealthy are some of your customers?

You know, the top 2%. I've served royalty.

Oh really? How did you know they were so?

Just found out, I didn't even know at first.

Royalty from where?

I won't say.

How about the bottom of the 98%?

I've served as high as the top end goes, but I've never really served as low as the low end goes. Like I said, average people.

Do you go to project buildings?

No, and I never would. As I said, if it was in any way an obviously compromised scenario or environment where I would be doing things, I wouldn't do it. That's not to say I don't take risks, because I do. Sometimes people come here [to my apartment]; that's a risk. People know where I live. I mean they are people I don't really worry about, but at the same time...

Have you appreciated the social aspect of the job? Has it inspired any of your photos or writing?

No, mainly because that's counterintuitive.

Not necessarily.

No, but it would be way more effort than I'm willing to put in it to make sure everything and everyone is cool with it. You know what I mean? It would be very interesting if I wanted to capture or document it, but it doesn't interest me. Also, I guess I have a level of shame about selling coke. I try to keep my interests separate because I don't like doing it. I feel bad selling coke. But, then, I don't have a moral issue…these people are already there. I'm not peddling coke to kids. I'm basically giving it to the guy who's already done it many times in his life. It is a cliché, but it's true: he would get it somewhere else.

Have you ever cut somebody off?

It's not really my place to do it, but a couple of times I've passed on information that this person is a little out of control.

Like calling multiple times in the evening?

Yeah.

What's the most a person has bought in one period in terms of dollars? $500?

Oh yeah, like $500 to $600. If you have a crew of people, that shit goes fast. I'm telling people sometimes that are debating, I'm like, "Look, you're with a couple of friends here; you're probably going to want a second one. It's better to get it now than call me again later."

Someone calling you over and over must be supremely annoying.

It is. I mean, I don't want to be a dick, but at the same time if it's too much trouble... I can't talk on the phone about it, I'm not going to get into an argument on the phone about it, and I'm not going to get into a long text argument about it. I just say "No, not now," whatever, leave it at that and hope that they get it. Sometimes I just have to shut my phone off.

Your phone bill records must get really thick in the early hours.

Not a lot of people have my number.

What, like a dozen?

Not even. I would say maybe six people have my number. Look, it's not smart, there's no question about it, I should get another phone.

If something bad were to happen, like if you were to get arrested while you were working, does you friend have a lawyer on retainer who would swoop in?

I don't think so.

Even for himself?

Maybe.

Do you guys hang out often, watch football?

Every once and a while we hang out, but generally it's just a business thing.

Do you worry about a customer ratting on you?

The people I deal with are only going to have one or two vials on them. If they get busted with one or two vials, I don't think the discussion turns to where did you get this from; the cops are like, "Oh, it's some blow." I think it would take a stretch for it to actually wind up in my backyard. Is that naïve? Perhaps.

WILL

30, Williamsburg

How did you become a heroin dealer?

OK, so I've been a heroin user for 13 years. When I first came to the city five years ago, I met this guy Keane—that's his street name—and he was a dope dealer from Baltimore. He was pretty high up on the food chain, so he would get ounces of crack and ounces of heroin. He had a brother named Paul, whom I met in Tompkins Square Park, just copping dope. He saw that I knew a lot of the local users around there, and he's like, "Do you want a job? Do you want to sell dope for me?" I was like, "I want to do dope, so I guess if I sell it I can make a profit and I can support my habit." So that's how that started. He would give me 100 bags, 10 bundles at a time—that's a sleeve. He would give it to me on consignment, and I was actually with someone who had a car at the time, his name was Mike. It was good dope so we gave our number out to a few people. I would always try to do it with people I knew, it was word of mouth, we never had business cards. Someone had to call for you and recommend you, then you yourself would have to call later. We would drive around and deliver—sometimes crack, too. We came into the whole coke thing later on because I got to know the guy better and he started to trust us more. So we started out with that sleeve. Most people bought a bundle, some people bought more—some bought five or six bundles.

A bundle is how much again?

In Brooklyn it's usually $70 or $80, but in the city it's always a flat $100. You usually don't deal with a lot of recreational users. And they're not straight-up hard-core users whose days revolve around it. They do spend money, though. When we had the delivery service, we got a couple disposable phones and had someone answering them doing dispatch. A buyer would call and say, "I need 17 minutes of your time," which means I need 17 bags of dope. "I'm at Second and 1st."

Mars Bar used to be over there.

Yeah, Mars Bar used to be right over there—we'd drink there and wait for more calls. It got to the point where we could work all day and night if we wanted to. He could drive and deliver at night, and I would answer the phones. Then, during the day, I would drive and he would answer the phones. I guess we always thought if they ever tried to tap the phone, or trace its location, he'd be at home sitting safe and I'd be out with all the dope. That went on for a good year. Then Mike fucked up at the bar, drunk, took his car off the highway and hit some kind of shit—just a really stupid way to fuck the business up. Then it became an on-foot thing. We had the same amount of clients, but we were just slower.

Would you take busses and trains?

No, we would just stop seeing people really far out and stick to a five- to ten-block radius. Or we had people come to us because we had really good dope and it was worth their time. That went on for a couple of months. We got even more strung-out because we kept getting more dope on consignment. It started out with a sleeve, then we would sell a sleeve in two or three hours. Ten bundles is nothing—somebody comes and buys five bundles in a go. At one point we were selling 40 to 50 bundles of dope in a workday that started at 9 a.m. and went to 5 p.m. We'd make $2,500 profit.

That's so much cash.

We were never sick; we always had extra dope. The cocaine came into play because people started asking for it. We started asking our guy Paul for it and he was like, "Yeah, yeah, I got a coke connect." It started out with dimes and 20s, and people really liked that. It was getting to the point where some people were just calling us for coke, like fuck that. If you're calling for $20-worth of coke, you're wasting our time.

It's only worth it if they're doing $50–$100 each time, as they were for heroin.

Right, it just wasn't working out, so me and Mike decided we were going to sell 50s of coke and 50s of dope. Usually people would spend $200, they would get two balms, or a bundle, and then two 50s of coke. That was worth it for us. Mike would do the calls, I would do the delivery, then we would swap it up after a couple of days.

Which did you prefer?

Doing the calls was a lot easier because I never felt like I was gonna get busted. I sat in the apartment, answered calls, and wrote people's names on a notepad. If there were already a couple people lined up and another called I'd tell them, "There's two people ahead of you, you got to wait." Then Mike would be on his way there. I'd usually try to line people up where I'd have them on avenues where Mike could walk straight up.

You'd get them at like Second and 7th...

Yeah, it would be 2nd Street, then the next guy would be at 5th, then the next guy would be at 8th—so on and so forth. I always stayed off the major avenues, because there's a lot of foot traffic, and a lot of police activity. There's just so much going on that even if there was someone watching you, you couldn't really tell.

You guys would always make the deals outside, in public?

I didn't; I don't know about Mike because he got himself busted twice in that whole thing, I guess by doing deals in public. I would go in a store, a deli, or a grocery or something, then walk down to the freezer and the person would walk down with me, then they would give me the money, I'd give them their shit. They would go out, I'd stay at the register, buy my drink, linger for a minute, see what happened. I always kept the dope in my underwear.

In your fly area?

No, I would put it under my nuts, 'cause sometimes the police are thirsty as hell. They'll take your pants, go all the way around your waist, shake your pants. They can't strip search in public, but if they have probable cause or they recovered drugs from someone else and the person says they got them from you, they can take you in and strip search you and all that. Once you're at that level, though, you're pretty much always busted.

You'd keep it against your naked scrotum?

Oh yeah, absolutely, almost against your ass. You don't want to lose it because that's a lot of money you're responsible for.

You're wearing briefs.

Yeah, briefs, I never really wear boxers. You don't want to lose your shit, it's very important not to lose it, but you don't want it out in public. That's why going into the bodega or into somewhere and doing the transaction is a lot easier and safer, because if there are eyes watching you, they have to come in to see the deal.

Would you be using heroin while running, and Mike while doing phones, and vice versa?

Mike used it a lot more than I did; I treated it like a job and I made a lot of money. I also didn't want to get arrested, which was a big part of it for me. I wouldn't get fucked up, I wouldn't be nodding out, dropping money. I've seen Mike get to the point where we would be waiting for more deliveries, and he would be getting high in the car, and I would have to come out. The phone would be ringing sitting beside him. I would just have to be like, "Dude, you got six missed calls, you got dope bags all over the car, like, what are you doing?" Mike was a good friend of mine, but he was just reckless. When I did deliveries and answered the phone and shit I used, but I didn't get fucked up.

I think a lot of people assume heroin addicts are either sick and vomiting or they're high as fuck and nodding out.

There's definitely an in-between, functioning middle ground. You got to use, because you have a physical sickness.

Do you still work with Mike?

No, that thing with Mike is done, so I suppose "hustling" is the day job. [Laughs.] I hustle whatever I have. Sometimes I'll find a bunch of books on the sidewalk, and if I recognize any good titles I'll take them to a used bookstore and make $20. I'll panhandle, I'll play music, I'll borrow my friend's guitar and go down to the subway and play whatever I can think of.

Do you have an apartment right now?

Yeah, I split rent with someone. I've been living there for about four months, and then before that I was living in a delivery truck I bought to travel with, so I wouldn't have to sleep on the street. Sleeping in that at night is like sleeping in a cave; some days I'd sleep till 2 p.m. and not even know.

Are you using a lot?

It comes and goes—right now I haven't used in five days. I'm on a methadone program. I drink the crazy juice. I don't like it at all, but after having a heroin addiction for 13 years, it's not a question of wanting to anymore, it's a matter that my body *can't* go without it. It's not sad because I made myself dependent on it, so yeah—it's my fault. But I don't sit around and cry and wish that I hadn't done this to myself, because I've met a lot of really amazing and talented people that are just fucked up mentally. They don't have good coping mechanisms so they use drugs to medicate. Every American has some sort of crutch, whether it be alcohol, porn, money, shopping—America's got your poison. But the only people I ever feel really truly sorry for are the people who lost the will to smile; you know, the people who are always constantly fucking depressed.

You've been five days clean. Why?

Because of the money. I have a big habit because I've used for so long. I also don't have a really wicked income right now, so I have to spread my money around a lot better than before. By taking the methadone, I can save money and I can pay more of my bills at my apartment. I can buy more art supplies, and I can put more money into creating things. It's not that I can't get the money; I hustle a lot of money every day, usually around $200 or more.

You're running around hooking people up?

Before that's how I made my high—by copping for people. I'd get someone a $100 bundle, but my guy sells it to me for $70, so I make $30 right there. Then to the next person I'd say, "Oh, I'll cop for you, but it's $100 and you got to give me three bags." If I'm not using I'd sell those three bags and then I'd have a total of $60. I could take that $60 and go buy a bundle then I could make $100 off of that. I can go from having nothing to a couple hundred in no time—if I'm not using the drugs myself. And then, of course, there are some days I only make $10.

Do you think you need to quit opiates to be happy in life?

No, I have to make more money. It's really a money game. What I need to do to support a habit and a lifestyle that I want is to find some saving ability and invest it. My problem is I don't have a consistent income. Without the ability to save, I can't really plan anything. That's my problem, 'cause I'm a writer and an artist, and I need to put more of my money into things that I care for and I am good at. I don't want to go get a job pushing a broom, and I don't want to wait tables—I don't want that shit because I won't last and if I do I'm going to be miserable. I'd rather make my talents and my abilities work for me. I need to put money into art supplies, into binding short stories, like, making a zine at Kinko's, instead of shooting all the profit.

If you're shooting dope I assume you're not in a place to write or create anything worthwhile.

Actually, I'm really good. Everyone is always better when they are clear and sober, but when I'm high I do find myself in a place where only heroin can take me. It definitely has its own beauty. The irony is in the things you only notice when you're high.

Did your friend encourage you to get on methadone?

Actually, he did. Even though I gave him money to spend, I think that he was jealous of my ability to get high, honestly. So he was like, "You should get on methadone to save money."

So you and your friend have each other's back when it comes to staying on methadone?

No, not at all. I'm just going to stay on methadone long enough to save enough money to fix my box truck. I was moving people's furniture on craigslist and shit. A regular moving company would charge you $700 to move a two-bedroom apartment, but I would charge people $400 or $500, just as long as they knew it was "at your own risk." Soon, once my moving service is operational, I won't have to hustle as hard as I do now, and I can have a consistent income.

So you're planning to go back to heroin.

Yeah, I will use again. I've been a user for so long, I'm probably a lifer. I don't see anything wrong with it, I think there just needs to be safer regulations from the government on how it gets into the country. That way people would stop dying from strange, fucked up poisonings. So yeah, there just needs to be more education about heroin—a lot more education.

THOMAS

37, Bay Ridge

How long have you tended bar?

I think I was 14 when I started my first job in a bar.

Have you encountered drug dealing in your bars?

Yeah, but most of the places I've worked in the past ten years have been old-time gin mills. We really keep drugs out of those places.

Why?

Eh, we're in the business of selling booze. These people are our customers; they're nobody else's customers. I just banned a guy for life a couple days ago because I caught him selling weed in the bar. He was in a corner and he had it right out in the open.

I was looking for it because he'd shown it to some people and they told me what he was doing.

He was going table-to-table showing stuff?

Yeah, pretty much. I mean, the guy was a jerk-off to begin with.

Have you ever thought about selling drugs?

Nope.

Why not?

Because I make a good living selling booze. [Chuckles.]

Are any of your regulars alcoholics?

Oh, without a doubt. We'd be out of business if we didn't serve drunks. But I mean if I don't get them drunk, the guy down the block is going to get them drunk.

That's how a lot of drug dealers talk. Have you seen someone over the years become an alcoholic?

Oh without a doubt. I mean I've told certain people I just won't serve them anymore. I'll let somebody else kill 'em; I'm not going to kill 'em.

How bad does a person have to get before you cut him off?

Eh, pretty bad.

How bad, like vomiting in the bathroom, sleeping at the bar?

I dunno. These days I just let people sleep at the bar because if they're sleeping I don't have to listen to them. I used to wake them up all the time and tell them they can't sleep at the bar but now it's just like, "Eh, if they're sleeping they're not causing any trouble."

Do you worry about cops coming into your bar and seeing that you're serving people who are visibly drunk?

Not really. I mean, we've got a guy who drinks at a bar down the street where the bartenders got so tired of him falling asleep that they duct-taped him to the barstool so he wouldn't fall off. Then they got tired of wasting duct-tape so they bought bungee cords to bungee him to the barstool. [Chuckles.]

How long would he be bungeed?

Three, four hours.

He would have to get up and piss?

[Wheezes, laughs.] Sometimes he'd do it right there in his pants.

Oh man. How old is he?

Fifty.

Shit. Where are his wife and kids?

They kicked him out a long time ago.

That's so sad.

Yeah, well. It's more important for him to have a beer and hang out with everybody than it is to hang out with his family. I mean, I got to work for 12 hours a day and for the first 11 hours I don't drink. I mean, I stand in front of 200 bottles of booze all day and it's no problem. Some people couldn't do that.

Do you enjoy the social aspect of being a bartender?

Oh, it's great. I like the people I meet. It's wildly unpredictable. I never know who's going to walk through the front door; it's exciting, it's fun. I'm 37 years old and I've never had a real job in my life. That's great.

What's a good book about the experience of bartending?

To be honest with you, for an English major I'm not much of a reader. But there was one book called *Cosmopolitan* [by Toby Cecchini] that's really good that one of my customers gave to me to read. It's about a guy tending bar in Manhattan in the 80s. It's less like *Cheers* the stupid TV show and it's a more realistic, day-to-day portrayal of a bar.

If you were alive during Prohibition, what would your

attitude have been about alcohol?

It'd probably be the same as it is now: I'd sell it.

But that would be illegal.

Yeah, well, I've worked at an after-hours… I mean, people go out and look for it because they want it. It pretty much sells itself.

Do you often serve cops?

All the time.

They're known as hearty drinkers.

Yeah, but schoolteachers drink more than anybody else, I think.

What are too many drinks in an evening?

I mean, that depends on how quick you drink them, who you are, and how you handle it. I mean, I don't think people should have a problem with drinking. My father drank beer, my uncles drink beer—guys drink beer. If you start fucking up with your family, if you start missing work—if it becomes a problem, it's a problem. I might go home and have eight beers, but that will be while I'm sitting in my recliner in my underwear from 7 p.m. until 3 a.m. I'm not anywhere near drunk because I'm only drinking one beer an hour. It sounds like a lot, but, you know. I got two kids; I don't really drink a lot anymore.

When's the last time you got really hammered?

Probably about a month ago. I'd just had a rough day at work. I had to break up a couple fights and throw a few people out. A woman hit me on the head with the receiver of a pay phone.

Jesus.

I had a knot in my head. She wasn't even a customer; she just wanted to come in to use the bathroom.

Did you drink those beers at home?

No, I just sat down at work and drank some whiskey and had a few beers.

Have you ever fallen off a stool?

No.

Have you ever vomited from drinking?

Not in over 20 years; not in my adult life.

Have you ever taken a break from drinking?

Yeah.

What inspires the dry days?

Maybe if I think I'm drinking a little too much, but these days I really only have just a few and that's it. If I'm working it means I'm working 12-hour days and I won't have my first drink until 4:30 a.m.

Do you think it's problematic if someone gets drunk seven nights a week?

I think it is with two kids. I think if you're 22, 23 years old, that's what you should be doing. Then you grow up.

What are the warning signs of someone becoming an alcoholic?

I think it's a matter of when going out and having a drink is more important than other things. Like, if my kids aren't feeling well I might go four or five days without a drink because I might have to take them to the doctor first thing the next morning. In that scenario I won't even think about not having a drink.

Do you have alcoholics in your life?

[Long pause.] Yeah, I have some family members who drink way too much.

How do you know they're alcoholics?

Just because they're drunk, constantly.

Which goes first, the brain or the liver?

I don't know, honestly. Probably the brain I'd say. People

become disconnected in conversations and stuff like that.

Do you think you'll ever need to quit drinking?

No. It's never been a problem for me.

Have you ever thought I was drinking too much? When you worked at O'Connor's?

Nope. You always maintained yourself.

Even when I would come in on a Sunday, and then on Monday at 10 p.m., maybe I'd stay until 1 a.m. I'd be drinking beers and whiskies. Maybe I'd have four sets of those.

No, I never thought you were. [Pause.] Did you?

Yeah, I wondered. I still wonder at which point I'm drinking too much. The thing is, I'm getting really good at drinking.

It's all right to have a few drinks. Do you put having a beer in front of other things?

Sometimes. It wouldn't be uncommon that I would leave the bar seeing double or I'd be walking in a not-straight line. My evenings would've been better spent reading books.

I mean, when you go to a bar it's not just about having drinks. There is the social aspect where you're meeting other people, having conversations.

How bad would I have to get for you to tell me to chill out?

I dunno. You could do something really stupid or keep getting banged up and not show up for work for several days in a row.

How about if I just insist on having the same conversation with you each time I came to the bar? Would you tell me I was doing that?

Naw. You'd be surprised how many people do that, whether they're drinking or not.

You won't let someone know you had that exact same conversation with them last night?

No.

Why not?

If that's what they want to talk about, that's what they can talk about. I'm there to listen, I'm not there to tell people what to do.

So I guess you gauge alcoholism in terms of creating problems instead of as a compulsion to drink.

Sure, I mean who doesn't like to have a cold beer on a hot day?

How about eight of them in rapid succession?

If you don't have anything to do the next day, you don't have any responsibilities, then why not?

When does a heavy drinker become an alcoholic?

I don't know. I don't think of people in terms of that. I mean, people have different rules of alcoholism. If you read the AA rules of an alcoholic it's like three or four drinks! You know, a lot of people have a few beers because they just came out to see their friends. One of the places I work we get retired guys who are 70, 80 years old coming in seven days a week. What are they going to do, sit at home and stare at the wall? They'll sit here for seven, eight hours and they'll sip on small beers and they never get drunk. They hang out with their boys and they watch the ponies. That's not a bad thing.

KRAMER

32, Williamsburg

Do you like being a drug dealer?

Whoa, right out the gate! Let me think on this one.

OK, so to back up a bit: you work for a marijuana delivery service. How long have you worked?

I've worked four days a week for the past five years, with no time off except for a week when I go to Puerto Rico. I call in sick about once a year, maybe twice. Sometimes I wake up an hour late, but I'm never too hungover to get on my bike and bust my ass. When that happens I worry the shit out of my boss because, since I'm usually so reliable, he assumes the worst—that I got arrested or hit by a car—and calls 311.

Not unlike a real job.

This is as real a job as any others I've worked, which is something I end up having to explain to friends: I work certain hours on certain days, and when we're hanging out outside that time frame I am not going to have weed on me to sell, just because my day-job is selling weed. You might as well be asking your friend who works at Wendy's for a cheeseburger when you're at the beach.

You're not the kind of pot dealer whose identify seems tied up with the trade and the stereotypical, 420/stoner culture. No Phish t-shirts or tie-dye in the rotation, I take it.

[Laughs.] Yeah, definitely not. I don't think I would know a Phish song if I heard it, to be honest. Although we're paid on commission, I essentially clock in and out. When I'm not working I really like walking around knowing that I could be stopped and frisked and not go to central booking.

Have you been stopped and frisked?

Twice actually, even though I'm white—don't think you have to be black or Latino to know firsthand how fucked up and scary it is to get run up on by plainclothes. Essentially you're getting jumped by thugs with guns who kidnap you for a while and will hurt you if you protest too loudly. And they take your weed and money, so it's a robbery.

Tell me about the first time you were stopped and frisked.

I was on the Upper East Side while I was working and I got arrested and booked. The stop was completely illegal. The other time I wasn't even working, I was in the back of a black Town Car, which the cops pulled over. They only questioned me, told me to get out of the car, and frisked me. Luckily I didn't give myself up; I had a used one-hitter in my pocket. Technically in a stop and frisk cops can't fish in your pockets for anything that doesn't resemble a weapon, but they can try to sweat the shit out of you by repeatedly asking you to show them anything illegal you have on you. Because I know my rights I walked away that night.

So do you like being a drug dealer?

Hmm. OK, I have to make a distinction between being a "drug dealer" and selling weed, because while I do do that in Manhattan, I resent the stigma. I'm grateful for the job, though, since the unemployment rate is still so high. There are people who would want to slit my throat for not working a job where I get a great workout on a bicycle for $200 to $400 on really insane days, paid in cash at the end of every day. I keep the money inside the turkey bag with the weed and it absorbs the smell. I once bought a couch at a furniture store with cash and the woman clerk started blushing. She was like, "Hey, Omar, come smell this money; it has a nice fragrance!"

That's cute.

I was uncomfortable. It took luck for me to be offered this job and balls to take it. But talk to me in a month's time and I might be crippled because a drunk driver hit me and took off.

—Or in jail.

Or in jail, I guess, but when most people say "jail" they mean central booking instead of Riker's.

What makes you think you wouldn't go to Riker's?

My boss pretty much guaranteed we'd never do jail time for working for him, even if the feds were working this whole time to build a case against him.

How do you know you wouldn't be included?

I've asked my boss about that and he said that maybe initially our names would be included in the investigation but he said he would have his lawyer take care of it, and that runners would never do jail time.

But how do you know that for certain?

OK, I don't know that for certain, but my boss does have a really good criminal defense attorney on retainer. I could tell you his name and you would probably have heard of him.

OK. That doesn't necessarily mean anything.

Maybe not, but every time one of us has been arrested—I won't say how many times or how many we are—our boss's lawyer has been there as soon as we get to night court. Literally four hours after anyone has gotten arrested our lawyer was already aware and working for us. But you know what? Even if it was possible we could get indicted in a federal investigation—I guess that's what it would be, right?—I can't afford to not work this job. I literally cannot afford to be dissuaded from this job—for the time being.

Your boss sounds interesting. Do you think he'd let me interview him?

I told him what you told me about this book you were doing and he said it was a "dry-snitch" book.

As opposed to a "wet-snitch" book?

I mean, I guess. He was just saying that there's a certain pride or obligation, more like, to keep secret about this industry. It's his only interest at the end of the day. But he said I could do your interview—as long as it's anonymous and doesn't say anything that could ID him. He did say he was interested in reading it though.

You are both getting copies. How did you get this job?

I guess I was recruited because I was asked to come talk about something. I thought I knew what that something was but that something was not just managing a couple pagers, a Rolodex of phone numbers, and a burner phone; that thing was actually riding the bike and answering texts from a dispatcher.

How much does dispatch make?

$150 a day, which is up $50 from what it used to be, partially thanks to me. When I first got arrested my boss took me off the streets because he didn't know if my face would now be familiar. Some of the phone guys traded for days on the bike, so there were phone days I could work, but for only $10 an hour. It wasn't worth it. I told my boss that I really didn't want to leave the serve but I was going to have to if phone days didn't pay better. I said I couldn't afford to stay. I was his first runner to get arrested and I think he wanted me to stay nearby, so he upped the phone day to $150 and I did that for a month before he decided I could work again—his lawyer told him it would probably be fine. I bought an entirely new bike, an unassuming backpack, and I started wearing collared shirts. Initially I resented not being able to wear my cut-off Dickies and metal t-shirts but now my day-to-day look is more preppy.

Do you like your boss?

Yes, I do; I respect him. He's fair, he doesn't play favorites among runners, and he takes the whole crew out to really expensive dinners for our birthdays. He also pays us a Christmas bonus—last year he gave me $800. That said, I wish we got paid vacation days, but I'm not about to start a union.

What was your job interview like? Did you have one?

Yeah, it was a real sit-down meeting at my boss's place. I was nervous; his place is elaborate, expensive, and weird. I remember sitting on a chair and being self-conscious about putting my beat-up sneakers on his really nice floor rug.

What was the interview like?

It was more him explaining exactly what he wanted me to do, which was to ride around Manhattan all day with a turkey bag of individually packaged cubes of weed and a flip-phone that would receive names and addresses. He asked me to work five days a week, which would make me well over $4,000 a month, and then I got really nervous. I told him I would just do one trial day and see how I felt. That day I made nearly $300, which did a lot to persuade me. Before that I was doing everything I could to get a job barbacking. Oh! But our serve's hiring policy is no girls, no non-white/Asian men, and no wild haircuts or elaborate tattoos.

Huh. Why no girls? It seems like they would be good at coming and going without being suspect.

True, they would, but the concern here is a customer raping her.

Oh.

The whole reason for being in that stranger's apartment is to deal drugs; a creep would know she probably wouldn't press charges. Also, my boss wouldn't want a runner getting raped because then he would feel compelled to set some precedent, but what would he do? Hire a goon to go attack the rapist? It's just a nasty route to go down.

Why no non-white/Asian men?

Sadly, because the NYPD stops and frisks blacks and Latinos a hell of a lot more than whites and Asians. A clean-cut Chinese guy in a button-up shirt and slacks? He might as well be a white guy; cops don't assume he is selling drugs when he gets buzzed into a brownstone. That said, we did have a black guy work for us for a few months. He never got stopped but he ended up skimming off the top and my boss had to fire him. He was also really slow getting around. I really like the guy; I miss hanging out with him when we pick up and I texted him as much after I found out he got fired. Oh, this is really satisfying, about excessive tattoos: I was once at a messenger bar and this guy, a friend of a guy I only kind of knew, asked if my serve was hiring. I was honest and said actually, yeah, but with your tattoos, you can't work for us. I mean, he had gnarly sleeves and hand and finger tattoos and shit on his neck, like cobwebs (which is supposed to mean you've been to prison, for Christ's sake) and Sailor Jerry, WWII bomber plane imagery. People who walk in and out of Park Avenue/Gramercy townhouses and mansions and Downtown high-rises don't look like that. I said to him, "In this case, your outlaw tattoos are preventing you from being an outlaw." He was put off but I could tell he knew I was right.

So do you like being a drug dealer?

As I said, as a job between careers I think it's great—maybe too well-paying because I'm not scouring other job listings. But I know in 20 years, when marijuana is legal all over the country, once states get hip to the billions in taxes they can reap in weed dollars, I will look back at this period of my life as probably the biggest adventure I ever had.

MCNEELY

46, Tremont

Holy shit, you're an NYPD cop and you used to work in the Street Narcotics Enforcement Unit [SNEU].

You want me to start with street narcotics? Well, it wasn't some mission where I felt I was going to be a caped crusader. The biggest appeal about it, most honestly, was having Saturdays and Sundays off so I could have fun with my friends. Also, it was dress-down, plainclothes—you're out of your uniform, which we call "the bag." I worked 4 p.m. to midnight. And there was some overtime pay because if any details came up you'd have to get back in the bag. When you had arrests, you pretty much were in court all the time.

As a drug cop, what kind of activity were you targeting?

Within the confines of a typical Manhattan neighborhood we

had two housing developments—which most people would call the projects—which were rampant with drug dealing and drug using. As a drug unit, we were going out there to find drug activity: who's selling, who's buying. During the four years I worked in this street narcotics unit, 85% of arrests made in our precinct were made in these housing developments. We were focused on individuals. We didn't run around and randomly throw people against the wall.

How did operations work?

You have an officer with binoculars and video equipment in position where they can observe "the set." You know who the dealers are—or as we called them "the players"—and you're in radio communication with your teammates in the field team. You're watching the activity and relaying, "OK, my player is on the set." After four years you know who all the players are, who's bringing the stash in from Uptown… Anyway, you have your buyers coming in systematically through the front door after someone buzzes them in. And the dealer doesn't think anyone in the world has eyeballs on him because it's the dead of winter, it's dark, so he's making hand-to-hand exchanges of small, hermetically-sealed bags of crack-cocaine—rarely would it be heroin. So as the observer you have an unobstructed view, you know your players, you take down the descriptions, and you witness the hand-to-hand. When you testify in court you're going to say, "I saw U.S. currency being exchanged for what was later deemed to be a controlled substance." You could have someone out there selling Comet or Ajax—everything has to go to the lab.

So if someone is selling fake crack it will be thrown out in court?

Absolutely, it's been done.

Even though there is an inherently illegal intention?

Yeah, and that would kill us. The district attorneys would say there is no way we can call this the sale of narcotics. It's very frustrating. We can say how the dealer went through all the gestures, how he took money for this substance and the buyer took it in his hand and went off with it.

Could the dealer be found guilty of fraud?

No, they wouldn't go that route. The DA would just drop the case because what he is being charged with and indicted with is a criminal sale of a controlled substance—CSCS. This man is charged with this crime and he is indicted. By the time the lab report comes back, he can already be arraigned and he's out, or ROR'd—released on own reconnaissance. No bail. He's not a bad guy; he doesn't have a record of dealing. So he's released, he gets a court date down the road, and when the lab report comes back and it's proven the fuckin' thing was Ajax, the case gets thrown out, simple as that. It doesn't matter what I witnessed.

You guys must know these players well—you spend time thinking about them, you study them. You know them by their full names, you know their personal histories and their families. Do you ever become fond of these drug dealers?

[Pause.] No, no. Me, personally, I never brought it home with me. But there was one player—a major player—who got under everyone's skin. This fucking kid was getting away with everything: Ralphie. Ralphie was just a filthy, horrible human being. He was one of the major crack dealers of the time. He had guys running stuff for him. He was making a lot of money, but you would never know it. When we were eventually able to secure a search warrant for his apartment, we thought it was going to be the greatest thing because this kid was driving the most expensive motorcycles with the $1,000 leather jackets, the gold, the earrings, he's got the $600 Air Jordans on his feet—the whole look.

Did you like his clothing style?

No! No, no, no. He repulsed me because I know he had his mother dealing crack for him. She looked to be in her 80s but it turned out—hard life—she was only in her 60s. What kind of person is going to jeopardize his mom, knowing how hot that area was at the time? People were being picked up every other night, both dealers and buyers. Sure enough, we locked his mother up. Ralphie had no virtue whatsoever. Other dealers might be different, who knows, but this kid in particular [scrunches up face]. He would make the runs Uptown, too. We didn't have the resources to put a tail on him, but we had an idea through the confidential informants that he was going to somewhere on 125th Street in Harlem. You know, I don't know if the kid smoked crack himself. I don't think he did. I know he smoked a lot of blunts. A lot of weed.

Good weed?

Yeah, smelled like it, but always in a Phillie Blunt. You'd go in the projects and see the remains of blunts everywhere. They're spending the money on the weed; they're not going to wrap them in Cuban leaves. (You can't touch cops with their humidors.) They're going to grab whatever is behind the counter at the bodegas, right by the cigarettes, dump that shit out and put in that good ganja, trees—back in the 90s we called it trees.

Oh, it's still called trees. You speak a bit fondly of marijuana.

No. I don't smoke it. You can't because of the drug tests. They're random. In the 20-year span of my career my number came up—it's your social security number—four, five times, and there was a mandatory test when I got promoted. My personal thing with marijuana is even when I could smoke it, before I became a cop, I didn't. I'm not saying it never will be, but it never was.

So you're saying you can't wait to retire so you can spark a big Phillie Blunt crammed with the best Sour Diesel available.

Peter, I am not saying that, [chuckles] but once someone is retired from a job, they have an option. At this point, there is no option—it is out of the question. I didn't like marijuana when I was young, I can't see how I would like it as a senior citizen.

The weed has gotten better.

Yeah? I'll get back to you on that one in a couple years, we'll do a follow-up! [Cackles.]

That'd be great. So what happened to Ralphie?

You do a lot of recon, you get confidential informants—guys who have been locked up too many times and they know the judge is going to sentence them to some jail, they'll do what we call a "flip."

They'll snitch. "Sing like a canary."

Cute. We call them CIs: Confidential Informants. They make deals with the district attorney's office, which is out of my hands. All I know is he is willing to give me information, and so he starts singing. In front of the district attorney we ask them, "What does Ralphie have in that house? Where does he keep the stuff? Are there kids? Dogs?" You cover everything because when you obtain a search warrant and a judge signs it, you don't want to make mistakes. There are horror stories all the time of cops hitting the wrong apartment, throwing grandmothers down on the ground and giving them heart attacks—whatever. When we finally got Ralphie it was because of diligent work. I couldn't believe the way this kid lived; his place was squalor. Squalor. Of course he had his 78-inch flat screen TV, but his furniture was milk crates.

Really? No $20,000 leather couches?

No, because everything outside of where he lived was for show, for the neighborhood. I equated it to the "White Lace" Irish in Boston in the late 1800s. They were all poor immigrants who lived in squalor but with whatever little money they could scrounge together they would get some nice lace curtains and put them in the window so when people on the street looked up it would look like they lived in a decent place instead of a shithole. So, with regards to Ralphie, I said, "Look at this white-lace motherfucka," with his mom living in there, a Pit Bull to attack anyone who would come in to rob them. This poor beast, when they raided the apartment and they threw the flash-bang grenade to stun and frighten everyone, that poor dog jumped out the fucking window! Don't worry, his apartment was on the first floor. I was happy because I'm an extreme animal-lover. I was like, "Run doggy, run!"

I have this preconceived notion that cops are across-the-board dog-lovers. What happened to his dog?

He got him back.

But you guys busted him.

The court systems here don't make these guys do fucking time! Everything is probation, probation, probation.

Tell me more about your binocular busts.

When I witness the hand-to-hand exchange, I wait until the buyer walks off the set, I get my field team on the radio and give them a detailed description, telling them he put it in his right pants pocket, along with his direction of flight, and they pick him up and toss him because now we have beyond reasonable suspicion to stop and frisk him. In his right-hand pocket he has four bags of crack-cocaine. Now we have probable cause to arrest the buyer, clink-clink. We let the dealer pick up a few more buyers because it's better for the case when it goes to court, but the whole time he'll be thinking, "OK, today's a good day!" Another buyer shows up on the set, boom-boom-boom, you see the exchange, my field team is now back in position, OK, the buyer is going south on this street, he's wearing this and this and so on, and we're just tossing bodies.

You mean tossing living, breathing bodies who are loved by their mothers.

[Smiles.] Loved by their mothers, yes. They would be very proud of them for buying crack on the street. One by one the field team is bringing the bodies back to the precinct until there are maybe four of them. Then we decide to call it a night and go get the dealer. When the dealer gets brought in, he's like, "Motherfucker, here are all the guys I just sold to."

Would the people living in the projects react to your SNEU operations?

Yeah, of course. You don't stop and frisk the dealer in the street because then everyone would go crazy, throwing stuff out the windows. They just hate cops. They hate us unless they need us. Then the first thing they do is call 911, but for things like an asthma attack or menstrual cramps, and now the fire trucks have to respond to that. I digress. Now, I'm going to tell you something and this is really fucking gross: There was one gang we called the "[project house name redacted] Red-Eye Gang." After you've arrested the dealer, you have to toss him in the station house, taking any narcotics, sharp objects, shoelaces, their belt because there are too many people killing themselves. So you're charging this guy with the sale of a controlled substance, but where is it?

Oh, no.

Oh, Peter, it's so nasty. I think the most we ever saw was 80 bags inside a bigger bag up his anus. Yikes. [Fists two salt and pepper shakers.] Give me two more salt and pepper shakers and that's how big it was. Ergo the name the Red-Eye Gang. Gross.

I always think of an asshole as a brown eye.

I dunno. Maybe people were bleaching them back in the day.

[Laughs.] This isn't a name they called themselves?

No, we were calling them that! You know, cops have a sick sense of humor, a *demented* sense of humor.

Did you ever tell these guys what their gang was known as?

Oh yeah, they knew!

Did they think it was funny?

Yeah, they'd laugh and be like, "You assholes."

This is a unique moment of cops and drug dealers communing.

Yeah, yeah. Back then not everything was on the computer, so you would have to spend hours writing out a report, fingerprinting with ink—

—Oh, they still fingerprint with ink.

Oh, no, not in New York. We're all on a system now that I believe is called LiveScan.

I have a friend who was arrested a year ago and they ink-printed him.

Where?

Nineteenth Precinct [Upper East Side].

Really? That just sounds so archaic, so primitive. I mean, I used to arrest prostitutes who would print themselves. There's not a cop in this department who could do better fingerprints than Sholanda, a prostitute. She was brilliant. I loved her.

But she was breaking laws all day.

Yeah, I felt bad for her. She worked without a pimp. She was probably the only one out of the hundreds of prostitutes we arrested—when I worked in a different department—who touched me. I once saw her when I was driving my private car on an off-day—even though I had tinted windows I could see her—and she was all beat up with a black eye. It was just a big egg. I pulled over and said, "Sholanda, you alright? What's up, girl?" And that is something I would never do because I was in my personal car. She kept her face covered with her hair and kept going. I was asking her to show me her face and to tell me who beat her up but she was too ashamed to look my way and she was barely talking. I felt bad for her, I really did.

Was she an addict?

I'm sure she was as I'm sure they all were.

As I'm sure you know, for the past 20 years or so, bicycle messengers work for marijuana delivery services. These guys service areas that span many precincts.

Yeah, they're not news to us. I imagine they don't get caught too often the way these bike messenger guys with the satchels weave in and out of traffic. The more mobile you are, the better. From my experience in what we just discussed, we're used to observing dealers who are locked in "a set," meaning you're staying in that spot. You're not moving around; they're coming to you. [Chuckles.] It makes my job much easier.

Dealers like Ralphie were selling 50 feet from their apartment?

Exactly. Ralphie sold right in front of his apartment.

So a word of advice to New York City drug dealers: be mobile.

Well, I'm not advising them to do anything of the sort. The only comment I'll make on that is: it's a good cover. A great cover. But if it's a Sunday night and instead of going into office buildings you're going into brownstones, yeah, someone is going to pick up on it. But then what are the cops going to do about that? There is a reasonable expectation of privacy in someone's home; you can't go in there.

Well, cops will just watch the guy lock his bike right in front of the brownstone, go up—presumably to sell weed—come down, and bust him.

No, they can't. How?

The plainclothes cops will flash their badges and say, "We're investigating burglaries in the area; what were you just doing in this building?" "—I just went to see my friend." "Who sees a friend for two minutes? What's his name, what apartment? We want to talk to him."

See, in that scenario you just gave, the cops didn't have any right to stop him. You gotta understand, especially now, there are levels of law…To stop somebody, if I go back to the Penal Law—"penal," haha—a cop needs to have reasonable suspicion. Once you have probable cause, then you arrest. With regards to my SNEU field team, I had reasonable suspicion to have my field team stop that buyer from a drug transaction that I observed. Now they can stop him and they can check his right-hand pocket because I saw him put the drugs in there. They go in his pocket, the drugs are in there, then it's probable cause and we can arrest him. You can research this yourself. I know you're very interested in this stop and frisk thing and it's controversial and it's in the news now. If I'm not mistaken, [the stop] has to begin with reasonable suspicion. You know, if someone is walking back and forth on a subway platform, a cop can't [legally] go up to him and say, "Give me some identification," but it's going to happen more and more because you have these young, inexperienced cops that are coming onto the job now, which is going to change the quality of officer you have out there. They're being paid this small amount of money. People will be like, "Fuck that. I'm not going to risk my life for that month's salary." You have to worry about the new crop of cop that is coming up. I mean in a report you have to articulate the reasonable suspicion to approach a guy and ask for identification. "Well, because this guy is walking back and forth like this." "What, furtively?" There has to be a reasonable suspicion that criminal activity is about to happen.

The thing is, my example of the messenger running up and down from a brownstone on the Upper East Side on a Sunday evening and getting stopped and frisked is something several people I know have said happened to them.

And the cops just went through his pockets? That case is going to get thrown out.

In one instance someone received an adjournment contemplating dismissal on misdemeanor sale of marijuana.

Sounds like a bad stop.

It seems unconstitutional.

Right. If he had a good defense attorney, it would have gotten thrown out and expunged from his record.

After a year it was. He even got back the $2,000 he had on him at the time, even though a cop working the desk at the station house said he'd get arrested at the property clerk's office if he asked for it. Have any attitudes you've had about drugs changed during your time with SNEU?

Well, the drugs changed! It went from crack-cocaine to this meth shit, which is crazy, man. You can Google the physical changes people go through—they look like zombies. Crack is whack, just like Whitney said. The weed thing? I dunno. You see more and more states legalizing it. In the penal code it's not even legally a controlled substance. It's a charge all its own: unlawful possession of marijuana is the charge.

Can a cop stop and search someone if they think they smell unburned marijuana on them?

Well, that's a grey area because a cop would have to articulate that. What if it's a rookie cop? How does he know what marijuana smells like? How many years was he in narcotics? How do you know that marijuana was in fact the smell emanating from him? Now, I would probably be able to articulate why and how I could stop someone with that smell, but if it was in an open area, how would I know it was that particular person? Me, I wouldn't go that route so I can't speak on that. I have personal experience because I went to training so I could do field-testing on marijuana. We used to have these little kits that we'd have right on the scene and we'd take a little piece of marijuana and put it in this little capsule with some kind of liquid and agitate it. If the liquid turned purple, it was marijuana. But beyond that, with all the legal stuff, you'd have to talk to the DAs.

If you had the power, is there anything about New York City's drug laws you would change?

Well, you had the Rockefeller Laws that were pretty strict, and then Giuliani came in and made it a more serious offense if it was within 1,000 feet of a school setting. You can do your own research on that. The only thing I would change is the possession of marijuana. I mean, I don't think people should be smoking it out in public because you don't have to be out in public to do that—you can smoke it in the privacy of your own home where you have a reasonable expectation of privacy. But marijuana doesn't lead to violent crime like cocaine or crack, when people get addicted to those and then they lose their jobs and then they have no way of making money—that's going to lead to crime because they have to feed their addiction. But I think it's a different thing with marijuana and I think it should be legalized—I really do. Don't you see it being legalized throughout this whole country?

Yes, I do. I think it will happen, as it has been, state by state.

Just like the gay marriage thing—finally that's picking up. But beyond marijuana, I think it's common sense to know that drugs (the hard ones that are addictive and mess with your brain cells) are going to lead to bad things. There are going to be guns and there is going to be crime and there are going to be robberies. It's just bad stuff when you're dealing with the hard drugs.

Was pot a common drug the SNEU team would bust people for?

No, it was almost always crack. 80/20 between crack and heroin. We didn't go out looking for marijuana, but let's face it, if you're walking around and you're a four-year veteran SNEU member, you're familiar with what's going on in the streets narcotics scene. You could be walking around in plainclothes and someone's burning one right in front of us, we'd at least issue the summons. But we concentrated more on getting the crack-cocaine dealers and trying to flip one of the buyers and have them make a deal with the district attorney and become a confidential informant. You make him a CI and then he brings you onto bigger and better arrests. You don't want to just keep arresting the users that are out there who are probably harmless, you know, they're a mess because they're addicted. Let's go up the chain, here; let's get the dealer. Where is the dealer getting his stash? The only way you can infiltrate that is with an undercover who is really good like Serpico, you know, a guy who really lives the life and can get all this information out. But on the smaller scale with the SNEU teams, you get a buyer and you take him into a separate room, you get him a sandwich—

—And this is what you would personally do? You are very trained in the art of persuasion, interrogation, and turning somebody?

Yes. Yes, flipping.

Have you ever felt bad corrupting someone's loyalty to the dealer?

To the dealer? No, I don't feel bad. That's on their conscience. These CIs are looking out for themselves. They're the ones who are being given the get-out-of-jail-free card for their information, and that's between them and the district attorneys. My role is only to ask if they are willing to speak to the district attorney for some leniency in their case. And if they're like, "Hell, yeah! I don't care. I can't go back. This would be three strikes for me and I would get serious time for this. Let me talk to the DA," the DA talks to this person and decides whether he's just bullshitting. Then it comes back to us to do the recon on the place, to determine whether all this information he's given us is credible, does this apartment face this way, blahblahblah. To answer your question about whether I feel guilty about flipping somebody? [Voice rises.] Absolutely not. He should feel guilty because he's flipping on somebody to save his own ass. We'll ask someone if they want to tell us who they're getting their stuff from and they'll say, "Get the fuck out of my face. Pig." "Alright, whatever. You want a candy bar? Get back in the cell." We'll take the next one out. "How's it goin'? Who'd you get it from?" "Fuck you." "OK, fuck you, too. Back in the cell." But then you'll get that one guy who will tell you the judge told him if he got caught one more time he'd be fucked, and he'll say he'll tell you anything you want to know. "OK, then. Let's go Downtown."

Yikes. Is it possible for a confidential informant to ever become a cop? Like, he's such a good spy that you guys say, "Hey! Put this guy on!"?

[Laughs.] No, probably not, although it's a clever idea. I think usually at that point in a person's career of using drugs that they'd have such a criminal record... Well, first of all, no one is supposed to enter the police academy who's been convicted of a misdemeanor or felony.

How about if a misdemeanor charge has gotten expunged? Do cops have access to that information?

Oh, yeah. That goes to the applicant processing division. They can find out if you had a ticket for an open container when you were 16 years old. But you would have to speak to someone who works in applicants. They do all the background checks on candidates at the police academy, and they can pretty much find out anything. They have to! You have to know who you're putting in your police department. But that's a funny question. I never thought about someone turning their life around to the extent they'd want to become a cop.

It seems the street knowledge that a drug dealer acquires would translate very well.

Well, you see, this street knowledge is what CIs use as a tool when they get locked up. But then down the road, when that same CI gets locked up again but at a different precinct, he's going to tell the officer to call officer so-and-so at such-and-such precinct… So I hear that my CI is locked up at the 2-0, which means I gotta go up there and take him to the DA. He's always going to be a CI, which means he is always going to rat on his dealers because he's paved the way for himself to be a recreational user of drugs for the rest of his life. I mean, it's not like he won't ever do time or he won't ever get arrested again, but the scales will always tip in his favor because the cops will always want the dealer over him.

He's will also be getting his ass kicked a few times, eh? Seems like a bad rep.

I'll tell you, in some of these projects we've known, if a CI gives someone up, he's in real serious danger. That world is very hush-hush. I don't know where you'd ever find a CI to interview, but it's safe for me to tell you that CIs are not doing it because they've had a change of heart and want to be on the right side of the law. It's always to just have that get-out-of-jail-free card in their back pocket.

Have any of your prisoners suffered from Stockholm Syndrome and they want to be your friend?

There's no period of time for that to ever happen.

At the station house?

But you're only there for three hours—tops.

That's still enough time for some back-and-forth banter.

No. A cop leaves them to themselves; you have too much paperwork to do. Now, people can go through the system a lot faster, but you have a few prisoners in a cell—it's never a one-on-one thing. Back in the day you were doing paperwork and fingerprints this high.

Even when it's three in the morning on a Thursday night?

I'm doing paperwork and they're sleeping.

You have to concede it's possible for back-and-forth banter to occur between cop and prisoner.

No, I do not have to concede that. [Guffaws.] I cannot agree with that whatsoever. Who you need to talk to is a correctional officer who works where they're housed. Now, that's a whole different thing. The COs aren't doing any paperwork. In my case the extent of interaction goes like this, "Hey!" "Whaddaya want?" "I'm starvin'." Alright, I'll get you a candy bar." You're too busy to have idle time and chitchat. The arresting officer can't wait to get rid of them.

Well, how about Sholanda, that prostitute you spoke of having a fondness for? You guys must have had some brief exchanges.

No. But Sholanda really hit home for me because when [we had her in the cell in the station house] she would shut the other ones up. Suppose you had ten of them at one time: waa-waa-waa-waa. They were always griping about something. I mean, they're fine surviving on the street but as soon as you arrest them they need to go to the hospital, they got to go to the bathroom, they're starvin' and they need a chicken parmesan or a pork chop. I mean, someone will be asking for a sauna when she hasn't taken a bath in three days. But Sholanda, because she was seasoned and older than these girls, would shut them the fuck up. She'd always say, "If you're hoeing, you're going—that's it." I mean, she would fingerprint herself because she just knew that if you're out there and you get picked up, you're going through the system and this was the game we played. She'd be out there tomorrow doing the same thing but she never gave you a hard time. We'd be five cops trying to get a ton of paperwork done, and she'd make me laugh. And we would take care of them; you know, we'd get them food and stuff. But that's a whole different thing.

Out of your own pocket?

Oh, yeah.

That's nice.

It is.

So what came of that instance when you saw Sholanda on the street all beaten up?

She just kept walking, and I didn't see her for a while. In fact, I don't know if I ever saw her again. I may not have been in that unit anymore, but the time definitely came where I wondered whatever happened to Sholanda. I definitely respected her. But I can't say that about anyone I encountered on the streets working on SNEU.

No charming drug dealers to speak of?

No.

No?

No. I just can't take that home with me. I can't go that route.

Is it a matter of not being able to afford to start investing yourself in who these drug dealers are as people? As human beings?

There's just no time. I don't think you realize the process of how fast it's in and out of the station house. We want them in corrections' arms because then we're not responsible for their safety or anything.

When this book comes out do you think I should worry about waking up one morning to the NYPD knocking on my door, wanting information about these anonymous drug dealers, or is that just me being paranoid?

That depends. You gotta make the details vague to protect us, but I doubt you'll be contacted you know, because the freedom of speech. You have every right to protect their identity. But that would be interesting if the NYPD wanted to know who these guys are. I mean, you talked to these drug dealers about their operations?

Yeah.

[Chuckles.] Be careful, Peter—Big Brother is watching. But I mean, what are they going to do, drag you to court and hold you in contempt if you don't give up your sources?

That has happened.

I know it has. Just keep it vague, especially with your little bike couriers there. It's a brilliant cover. Just don't be specific, especially with me. If I was retired I wouldn't give a shit but I have to secure my pension. But I don't think I'm doing anything wrong; I mean, I'm entitled to my opinion.

I wondered if the NYPD ever works with the banks and the IRS to build RICO cases against drug dealers. How does that work?

Oh, I don't know. You mean in terms of dirty money?

Yeah, like someone building an empire, like how Al Capone got busted.

Or Scarface who had the men with the bags of money. You have to hide that money otherwise it will go to asset forfeiture and the IRS will get it. But that would be more of a federal thing. The NYPD might have liaisons, but that's too big for a local police force.

Hey, you know what? You could be a really good drug dealer once you retire!

I suppose so, but I'm what you'd call an old-schooler now that the technology has changed so much.

You could get out of a stop and frisk no problem. You know

how to play the game.

Yeah, but there is a different crop of cop out there today, a whole different breed. They're young and overly enthusiastic. And the NYPD—whether they admit it or not—are quota-anxious. They want these kids making these numbers. They want these kids making these stops.

They want them to make the stops that get thrown out in court?

Yes. The commanding officer is happy because they have something called CompStat once a month down at police headquarters. He gets credit for felony arrests even if they get thrown out, or "DP'd": declined prosecution.

Are you curious about these drug dealers I've interviewed? Do you want to bust their heads?

No.

You don't feel any ill will toward them? You don't think they're scumbags, cockroaches, bad people?

What are they dealing?

A lot sell weed. Some cocaine. Molly, Percocet, heroin.

You know, as long as these guys aren't pushers and they're not selling it to kids or they're not selling it to people who are selling it in schools… If their customers are consenting adults and they're not out committing crimes—like the marijuana thing, which I have no issue with—no, I don't want to bash their heads in. But how are they getting away with it so easily? I'm curious.

I don't know. But these weed messengers make $40–50,000 a year just selling weed.

Wow. Let me ask you this: Did you ask them about how they feel about the cops who lock them up? Do they want to bash their heads in?

Yeah, most. But I was amazed: there was one weed messenger who shared the same birthdate as his arresting officer who safe-kept his one-hitter and a dime bag of weed in his personal locker.

Wow! Wow.

This weed dealer was really touched.

Wow. I'm amazed. That sounds like something that would happen back in the day when cops would sample the cocaine. I can't picture that happening now, but bully for him. That's unique. That's a pretty cool story.

These interviews are anonymous, which means I've let sources choose their fake names and set the parameters of the photographs. I've also scrambled potentially identifying locations, ages, and dates.

First I must thank my varied, fascinating, and generous sources for trusting me with their stories (you know where I live). I would like to thank Athena for being so helpful, very (very) pretty and for offering invaluable advice. I am very appreciative to Arman Dzidzovic for his transcription work and camaraderie. Huge bear hug to Christy Karacas for creating such a supreme cover. Big ups to Eddie Huang and Kenzo Digital for their consultation and support. John D'Agata has been a cheerful and generous teacher to many. I thank Gavin McInnes for encouraging me to do interviews. I additionally extend gratitude, in no particular order, to: Josh and Noah (for turning on the faucet when they shit; I wake up otherwise); Brant, Dylan and Des, Steve, Manuel, Carl Hedrick (RIP), Ryan Henry at *Thrasher* for publishing my stuff; skateboarding, the proverbial Giving Tree; the readers of Word on the Street New York (let's make it a book!); Keith McCulloch; O'Connor's (RIP); Charles at Supreme; Charles Allcroft; Becky and Mike; Brian Kuzma, Sam McGuire, Mitch, and the eternal Full Kit crew (support your local shop!); Diana and Tamika; Dave Eggers, that *Believer* interview you did with Jack White about carpentry way back when forever changed my idea about the potential of interviews. No thanks: Baxter High School's deficient curriculum; Pam Creedon. I would like to thank Will Luckman, Craig, Wes, Krzysztof, and everyone at powerHouse for giving me a shot. And most of all, thank you, Fuzz, for being such an indispensable pal.

DEALERS

Published in the United States by powerHouse Books,
a division of powerHouse Cultural Entertainment, Inc.
37 Main Street,
Brooklyn, NY 11201-1021
T: 212.604.9074
F: 212.366.5247

info@powerHouseBooks.com
www.powerHouseBooks.com

First edition, 2013

Library of Congress Control Number: 2013940411

ISBN: 978-1-57687-647-3

Printing and binding by RR Donnelley

Book design by Krzysztof Poluchowicz
Cover design by Christy Karacas

A complete catalog of powerHouse Books and Limited Editions
is available upon request; please
call, write, or visit our website.

10 9 8 7 6 5 4 3 2 1

Printed and bound in China